Jesus vs. Jesus
The Christ, God's Word, God's Spirit Unveiled

By
Mike Bhangu

BBP
Copyright 2017

Copyright © 2017 by Mike Bhangu.

This book is licensed and is being offered for your personal enjoyment only. It is prohibited for this book to be re-sold, shared and/or to be given away to other people. If you would like to provide and/or share this book with someone else please purchase an additional copy. If you did not personally purchase this book for your own personal enjoyment and are reading it, please respect the hard work of this author and purchase a copy for yourself.

All rights reserved. No part of this book may be used or reproduced or transmitted in any manner whatsoever without written permission from the author, except for the inclusion of brief quotations in reviews, articles, and recommendations. Thank you for honoring this.

Illustrator: Mike Bhangu
Published by BB Productions
British Columbia, Canada
thinkingmanmike@gmail.com

I dedicate this book to the Christ.

Table of Contents

Preface
Introduction

Who is the Christ?
The Word and The Spirit
I Salute The Spirit
How God's Spirit Answers
God is More
The Trinity Unveiled
In the Beginning...
The Beautiful and the Ugly
Lost in Translation
Lost in Translation: Endnotes
Dialogue and Plot
Serpents, Doves, and Tricksters
Fool's Gold
An Enemy or a Friend?
The Cross and Jesus
Dead yet Alive
The Purpose of Suffering
The Pain of Jesus
Misunderstood Genius
The Missing Link
The Dead and the Living
The Body Matrix
The "I"
Jesus' Sacrifice
How to Die: Salvation
Is Jesus God?
Saving the Christian?
If no Jesus: Heaven vs. Heaven
If Jesus was a Mortal Man
Eggs, Bunnies, and Jesus

The Original Sabbath
The Sun God
God is Within
The Best Time to Pray
Son of God
The Tree of Knowledge
Why Sex is Sin
The Antichrist
The Beast
666
Succubus
Three Days
Conclusion

Appendix A: The Khalsa

Preface

I have no political agenda. I'm not out to disprove Jesus. Nevertheless, after many years of research and study, I'm unable to accept the literal and popular interpretation. It doesn't resonate with my reason.

In my understanding, with truth as the prize, there is more to Jesus and his story than the common version. Jesus and his story are much more powerful and revealing.

My inclinations do not stem from only one school of thought. The truth is absolute and identifiable in more than one house. It's a matter of understanding the symbols, terms, and context, and outwitting the hidden hand's many religious riddles and intentions. Moreover, it was only after delving into the different theologies and spiritual ways did I appreciate each more completely. One cannot be fully understood without the others. As such, the considerations I present travel outside the box of popular Christian thought and lift Jesus above the many counterfeit notions forced upon the flock. *Jesus vs. Jesus* is the outcome.

For some, the information I present will be difficult to accept. Yet, what is good is never easy. I only present knowledge able to help a person find and hold Heaven. In my interpretation, this information is hidden and further presented as something it isn't.

This said, I must confess, the truths I present are arduous for me to walk with. My hope is, someone reading is more capable than me and strong enough to embody them.

....

I did not invent the knowledge I share. In no way do I claim otherwise. All knowledge already exists. Sometimes, it's clear as day. Sometimes, it's allusive. And sometimes, it's buried underneath centuries of misunderstandings and political intentions.

"But woe to you, scribes and Pharisees, hypocrites! For you shut up the kingdom of heaven against men; for you neither go in yourselves, nor do you allow those who are entering to go in."
— (Matthew 23:13)

Introduction

For over 300 years, the Roman Empire hunted the Christian. Countless were tortured and executed. The Roman Empire desired to eliminate every Christian from the Roman dominion because the Christians were not easily ruled by Roman values, and the House of Jesus taught the common person the truths of the spiritual world. Spiritual truths can empower the people, and a powerful people might overthrow the status quo in favour of conditions that enhance their living standards. If this happens, the few who benefit from the divisions within society, the rulers, will lose their wealth, influence, and power.

Fortunately, the Roman Empire was unable to eliminate the Christians. Mystically, Christendom continued to multiply. With the killing of one Christian, two would rise to take his or her place. Persecuting the Christians only provoked the growth of the faith.

Unfortunately, the Roman ruling class employed another tactic when the first failed. They strategically infiltrated Christendom and redirected Christian intentions away from them. The empire embraced them, became them, and took control of them from within.

When it isn't possible to eradicate knowledge, the powerful will infiltrate the institution built to communicate that knowledge. From within they will manipulate the information delivered to the general public—concealing truths and popularizing information designed to misdirect the truth seeker.

Knowledge is power and to keep the general public ignorant, through multiple fronts, knowledge is destroyed, hidden, or distorted. Sadly, almost all popular religions eventually evolve into an instrument of the rulers to herd the ruled and to maintain their status.

The Roman Empire not only hijacked Christendom, this institution also merged Pagan ideas with Christian notions, so to appease the Roman Pagan population. This further obscured Christian truths.

In my interpretation, many early Christian writers were aware of Roman interference, and to ensure the truths of the invisible realm were passed to the future generations, they wrote in code. Ideas were written in such a way as to survive Roman scrutiny. Wittingly, they hid the treasure in full view of the enemy. It's beyond genius—it's beyond human ability.

Yet, to add to the religious riddles, Christianity experienced the European dark ages. It was a time of ignorance, and many codes and symbols were misunderstood by the people of then. Those misinterpretations are still with the Christian world.

Not all of *the New Testament* is written in an allegorical fashion. However, many important spiritual lessons are, and if correctly understood, the true nature of everything can be unveiled. This manuscript will decode many notions concealed within *the New Testament,* ideas such as:

- God's Word.
- God's Spirit.
- The Christ.
- How Jesus was God.
- How Jesus was the Son of God.
- The cross.
- The antichrist.
- The end-of-days.
- The nature of the beasts.
- The battle between good and evil.
- The secret of Jesus' resurrection.

The analysis I present contradicts the popular versions. You do not have to agree and I apologize if you're offended. This is not my intention. Know that I love Jesus. He was superhuman. There's enough literary evidence to support this. I'm only presenting what I think is true and relevant, even though it might sound incredible, and it's only after many years of digging through the religious rhetoric, do I share my knowledge. Perhaps, I'm completely incorrect and the popular interpretations are true. Take what I present as you will and judge for yourself.

Mike Bhangu

Who is the Christ?

The surname of the Nazarene known as Jesus isn't Christ. All Christian scholars will agree. The term, Christ, is a designation.

Over the past several years, I spoke with many followers of Jesus and most were unaware of the mentioned. Nor did they know what the term represents, and through no fault to them. Most of what they know of Jesus was taught by the churches. Sometimes, the churches facilitate a false narrative. Sometimes, the churches aren't even aware of it. Political insertions and motivations of long ago, pollute the majority of world religions and the many doctrines. Christianity isn't exempt. As such, today, the God seeker isn't privy to all of Heaven's truths, and falsehoods, presented as genuine, readily obstruct their spiritual voyage.

Jesus was superhuman and rightly given the title of Christ. But what is a Christ?

The term, Christ, if correctly grasped, is as a Philosopher's Stone. Through the knowledge of the title, the most-high spiritual notions can be understood and a person has a greater chance of resting in the Lap of God.

The word, Christ, can be granted to any person. However, most people will never taste the title. Only the select reach the required conscious awareness.

The crown of Christ is given to and rests on the individual in whom God's Word is awake and active. God's Word sits within every person and is dormant until a Divine intervention. However, only the perfect receive such attention. They are those who've killed the body but still live—they are those who've mastered the material and are slaves to the spirit—they are those blessed by God's Glance of Greatness.

Jesus was such a person. He was perfect. Captain of the physical and metaphysical—a saint-soldier with a perfect soul—a creature harmonized with all that is pure. Consider him Heaven's superhero. In him, God's Word was awake.

> *"The Word became flesh and made his dwelling among us." —* (John 1:14)

God's Word is another concept missed by many, and again, through no fault to them. Truths are hidden, the person is misdirected, and without understanding the meaning of God's Word, the Christ cannot be fully apprehended.

All popular religions teach that their Holy Book is God's Word and no other book can claim this honour. This includes Christendom. Each further suggests that the other religions are inferior. Nevertheless, the Holy Books do not associate The Word with the entirety of any Holy Book or religion. God's Word is misunderstood, and by extension, so is the Christ.

To add, the whole of a Holy Book consists of words and not just a single word. In the different books, within this context, when God's Word is described, it isn't pluralized. Yet, religions associate God's Word with words, sentences, and paragraphs.

> *"In the beginning was the Word, and the Word was with God, and the Word was God." —* (John 1:1)

God's Word as a collection of words doesn't really make sense. I struggled for many years hoping to rationalize the popular depiction taught by the different religions. I couldn't do it. However, outside the accepted notations, placed within the original context, God's Word is an easily understood phenomenon.

Yes, it's true and the phrase "God's words" is used in some of the Holy Books, yet, this doesn't reference God's Word. In addition, in *the Old Testament* and *the New Testament*, the notion of "God's Word" is applied in different ways and with different means—furthering the confusion. At times, it refers to what God supposedly said to a person, and at other times, it references God's Word as I present it. Moreover, it's evident that meaning was lost in translation and the English versions of the different Holy Books do not give the same messages as those in the original languages. My suspicion is that the original documents are much clearer as to what God's Word truly is.

God's Word isn't the whole of any Holy Book and God's Word is a sacred frequency/sound/vibration.

How did I come to this revelation? By recognizing that there is truth in every true religion and then independently travelling deep into the different religious literature. This said; the Sikh Holy Book, *Sri Guru Granth Sahib Ji*, was instrumental in teaching The Word as a primal vibration and revealing the common celestial thread linking every true religion. *Sri Guru Granth Sahib Ji* explicitly deals with concepts that are hidden in other Holy Texts. This Holy Book is akin to a key able to decode the other true religions. The Sikh Guru freely reveals what the mystery schools conceal. Without the teachings of the Sikh Guru, it might've taken me several more decades to grasp the concepts I present, if at all.

Unfortunately, the popular notion of The Word, amid the Sikhs, as the others, is also wrongly linked to the entirety of their Holy Book. Sometimes, what is written isn't what's popular.

> *"The Unstruck Sound-current of the Shabad, the Word of God, vibrates in the Court of the Lord."* — (Sri Guru Granth Sahib Ji, ang 1137 of 1430)

> *"When the body dies, where does the soul go? It is absorbed into the untouched, unstruck melody of the Word of the Shabad (God's Word)."* — (Sri Guru Granth Sahib Ji, ang 327 of 1430)

The Word of God is a sacred frequency/sound/vibration. The Word resonates within everything that exists and is responsible for setting the whole of creation in motion. Everything that exists is in a state of vibration, and without this sacred frequency, nothing has a constitution.

> *"...that by the word of God the heavens were of old, and the Earth standing out of the water and in the water."* — (2 Peter 3:5)

A theory of Quantum Mechanics, *String Theory*, suggests that extremely tiny string-like particles pervade and vibrate through everything within the Universe. The characteristics of these strings are very similar to the characteristics given to God's Word.

When you read the different Holy Books, without the misdirection, "God's Word" is described as I present it. What's more, The Word understood as a collection of words and sentences doesn't allow the mind to comprehend many doctrinal passages. Take the following as examples. They make little sense under the popular definition but are easily grasped if applied as a sacred vibration.

> *"For the word of God is alive and active. Sharper than any double-edged sword, it penetrates even to dividing soul and spirit, joints and marrow; it judges the thoughts and attitudes of the heart."* — (Hebrews 4:12)

> *"The grass withers and the flowers fall, but the word of our God endures forever."* — (Isaiah 40:8)

The Word is in every person but rests until awoken. When fully active within the body fortress, the person becomes one with "All" and becomes "Christ", and simultaneously, inherits the supernatural abilities that accompany the activation. Accordingly, Jesus was not the only Christ to exist. Others too were blessed with The Word. Nanak, Moses, Enoch, Buddha, and Hermes Trismegistus (Thoth) are some of the other lucky persons.

When The Word is awake within a person, a purification of the mind and body pursue. He or she rises above the faults and duality of the body. Herein, the influences of the body no longer communicate to the time and space of thought. As a result, the spirit is released and becomes the dominant source of information influencing a person's thoughts and actions. Since the spirit is the conduit to The Father, in such a state, a person is in harmony with God's Will. The Source flows through him or her.

The Word, or what Laozi, also known as Lao-Tzu, called "Tao", is unbelievably powerful. When active, the vibration unlocks salvation, unlocks nirvana, and unlocks the all-in-one medicine for every ailment. Moreover, the consciousness expands to incorporate the unconsciousness and the two halves of a person become one—the higher-self and "this self" unite, and the invisible and the visible are simultaneously perceivable by a wake mind. It is the meeting of the groom and the bride.

> *"Wherefore lay apart all filthiness and superfluity of naughtiness, and receive with meekness the engrafted word, which is able to save your souls." —* (James 1:21)

The subtle nature of all that exists is known by those The Word is active within, and through The Word, the subtle nature can be influenced. A change in the subtle translates into a change in the physical nature of a thing, and this is how men like Jesus performed miracles such as healing the sick, walking on water, raising the dead, and multiplying bread. They modified or corrected the blueprint (the subtle) to bring about a physical modification or correction.

Everything in existence was first conceptualized by The Great Architect. Then it manifest as a metaphysical thing—spirit—blueprint. After which, the physical evolved from the subtle. Consequently, all material things exist within the parameters of their subtle essence. The mystics of the world, past and present, are able to perceive the invisible nature of existence, and able to influence this essence.

The invisible component to everything that exists occupies the same space as the material. If a mystic wishes to manifest matter or influence a material thing, he or she first manipulates the subtle essence. There is a correlation. A change in the subtle effects the physical and vice versa. To manifest matter, the mystic first creates the subtle essence and then the physical naturally comes into existence.

The title, Christ, was given to Jesus because God's Word was fully awake and resonating within him. This is what John meant when he wrote, *"The Word became flesh and made his dwelling among us."* (1:14)

This interpretation of the Christ isn't popular and I believe it initially was—particularly, amid the Gnostics. During the very end of writing this manuscript, I was introduced to the 13 books that constitute *the Nag Hammadi Library*. After a very brief glimpse, one of the books in this Christian Gnostic collection literally presents The Word as I present it.

It's also my belief that the contemporary low-level priestly class unintentionally misdirect the lover of Jesus. They teach handed-down information that doesn't instigate a complete thought. The same isn't true with the elite priestly class and they're fully aware of what the truth is and what's designed to misdirect.

Now, why is the common person misdirected from understanding the notion of God's Word and the concept of the Christ? It's simple. Knowledge is power and the most powerful are spiritual truths. God's Word and the understanding of the Christ can transform a sheep into a Heavenly lion capable of overturning the status quo, in favour of supernal laws. For this reason, to protect the power structure, truths are concealed.

I might be wrong and no agenda as this exists. It might be that the misunderstandings rest at the very top of the power pyramid and inadvertently propagated as absolute. Whatever the reason, there is more to *the Gospels* and the story of Jesus. If a person can comprehend his spiritual journey, John 14:12 too might reveal its vagueness.

"Verily, verily, I say unto you, He that believeth in me, the works that I do shall he do also; and greater works than these shall he do; because I go unto my Father." — (John 14:12)

God's Word isn't the whole of any Holy Book and God's Word is a sacred frequency/sound/vibration. In Jesus, the Christ, God's Word was fully active.

....

During my research, I stumbled upon an interesting lecture by Santos Bonnaci, titled, *Elixir of Life*. In the presentation, Bonnaci is explaining the physical reaction to the secretion of a particular fluid within the brain. This fluid supposedly heightens a person's awareness and abilities. Although Santos doesn't suggest this, it's my belief that he's describing the physical reaction to the activation of God's Word. *(Naturally, as with the other researchers I cite, just because I agree with one or two ideas, this doesn't mean I agree with all their conclusions and associations).*

Mike Bhangu

Jesus vs. Jesus

The Word and The Spirit

After spending many years examining religions, I was blessed with a revelation, the awareness of God's Spirit.

God's Word purifies by eliminating the egoic and material identity of a person. This allows the spirit within to rise and direct the thoughts of a person.

The spirit is conscious of God and the spirit acquires its direction from The Lord. A person walks in the Will of God when The Word courses through an individual.

The power of The Word (The Shabad) is indescribable and from The Word comes all creation, within all creation is The Word, and in The Word all merge. The Word can even reanimate the unanimated—what most people might denote as "raising the dead". However, within a person, the sacred vibration is silent and must be triggered to sound.

The Word is alive but dormant until awoken and only God reveals God's Word. In specific, God Spiritually-Manifest. God is said to be Unmanifest and Manifest, and the Holy Spirit is the name given by the Christians to identify the second.

A common understanding there is amid the many religions, God is Unmanifest and God is also Spiritually-Manifest. The Great Architect is in all creation and all creation is in The Great Architect—the Unmanifest aspect. Simultaneously, God is unto the self, outside all creation, and interacts with God Unmanifest—the Spiritually-Manifest aspect.

The craving that each living thing has, the yearning for something—a union—a completion, commonly misidentified by the contemporary person with a love for a material object or another human, is an innate desire to reunite with The Unmanifest. This is why a material object or a person can't permanently satisfy the craving. A material object or a person only disguises the feeling, like a pharmaceutical painkiller. When the mind has grown accustom to the material object or person, the yearning will again speak to the time and space of thought. Only The Source can provide an unbreakable and everlasting love. Only The Great Architect can satisfy the inner impulse.

The idea of God Manifest is in almost all religions and in *the New Testament, the Old Testament,* and *the Qur'an,* the terms The Spirit, The Holy Spirit, and The Spirit of God signify God Manifest. The Sikh doctrine knows God's Spirit as Sat Guru. Thoth called The Manifest, Poimandres. The Buddhists know The Spirit as Maitreya.

Sometimes this notion of God Manifest isn't so easy to identify, and as author Alexander Smith suggests in his book, *The Holiest Lie Ever: Glorified by Myths, Mysticism, Symbolism, Rituals and Traditions,* the symbols of the dove and fire, at times, represent the Holy Spirit. These symbols can be found in a multitude of religions, including those of the ancient Greeks, the Romans, the Druids, the Egyptians, the Incas, the Hindus, the Buddhists, and the Celts, who claim their Salic Laws were guided by Sat Guru. The Celts named The Holy Spirit, Salo Ghost. Vishnu is the name given by the Hindu religion. Supposedly, this is a secret kept by the high caste Hindus—the Brahmins. But since I didn't learn from any clandestine school, I have no need to hide truths.

Although it might appear as if there are two, God Unmanifest and the Holy Spirit, there is actually only one. It's difficult to comprehend. A distinction there is and a distinction there isn't.

> *"For God has revealed them to us by his Spirit. The Spirit searches all things, even the deep things of God."* — (1 Corinthians 2:10)

> *"Without the True Guru (Holy Spirit), no one has obtained the Lord; without the True Guru (Holy Spirit), no one has obtained the Lord."* — (Sri Guru Granth Sahib Ji, ang 466 of 1430)

The potential to build a relationship with God Manifest rests with every person, but God Unmanifest cannot be found or understood solely by woman or man, and only God's Spirit can introduce a person to The Lord. Furthermore, God's Spirit is a teacher—the all-knowing and always truthful Professor. A lecture conducted by The Spirit will reveal reality's true nature. But only when the student is ready, will the teacher appear.

> *"We have not received the spirit of the world but the Spirit who is from God, that we may understand what God has freely given us."* — (1 Corinthians 2:12)

To connect with Sat Guru, a person should meditate towards, pray (produce the appropriate vibrations through sound), genuinely perceive all creation as one, sincerely beg The Lord, and function through the better half of the mind's duality. In one half of the mind live such things as love, truth, compassion, humility, and selflessness. In the other half live such things as lust, anger, pride, greed, and attachment. The human being is in a constant state of vibration and the frequency changes to correlate with a person's thoughts, behaviour, and emotions. If a person dominantly operates through the better half of the mind (further discussed in an upcoming article), their constitution will produce a resonance The Holy Spirit favours and their subtle essence will attract the spiritually pure principles. Such a person is in a state of being ideal for a celestial experience.

> *"For the sinful nature desires what is contrary to the Spirit, and the Spirit what is contrary to the sinful nature. They are in conflict with each other..."* — (Galatians 5:17)

If a person functions through the negative aspects of the mind, such as anger, lust, attachment, pride, and greed, a person emanates a vibration/aura/frequency that doesn't impress Salo Ghost.

Suppressing the ugly half of the mind's community isn't easy. It's a great sacrifice. It's overcoming nature. It entails great internal pains. People as Jesus, with every waking moment, were able to control anger, pride, attachment, lust, and greed. Regardless of who was insulting him, or the ugliness of the slander, or how much anger he was shown, Jesus didn't let such things as anger and pride get the best of him. Never mind the worldly wealth, all earthly kingdoms were offered to him but Jesus controlled his greed and rejected the material realm.

Almost every human being daily falls to their body's influences. As much as a person might know better, when the body's influences speak—when the units of information such as anger, lust, attachment, pride, and greed communicate to the time and space of thought—almost every person fails. The individual will probably overcome many of the low-level impulses sent by the body, but most people cannot, moment-to-moment, overcome the units of information when they speak at their loudest. The impulses sent at full strength are very powerful and they have a habit of dominating the time and space of thought.

If one continues progressing, by the Grace of The Father, eventually, silencing the beautiful half will also become a requirement. Both aspects of the mind's community are connected to the body and are linked to Mammon/Maya. The body must be completely silenced for the spirit to rise. However, I'm not suggesting that love isn't a characteristic of those who've triumphed over the body. When the spirit is king, a different type of love is given and experienced. It's pure.

Jesus controlled his body's influences and his reward was the correct vibration. The vibe he produced attracted the attention of The Holy Spirit.

> *"And Jesus, when he was baptized, went up straightway out of the water: and, lo, the heavens were opened unto him, and he saw the Spirit of God descending like a dove, and lighting upon him."* — (Matthew 3:16)

The authority and instruction of The Holy Spirit is necessary to understand The Great Architect. Without Sat Guru, no person will truly grasp the wonders of The All. If a person were to forget all religions and entrust strictly in The Holy Spirit, they will gain enlightenment. The Holy Spirit taught all the true sages. For that reason, religions have much in common. The source was the same and the differences are Earthly assertions.

The Perfect Guru teaches the person and no individual can truly understand the nature of reality without The Holy Spirit. But God's Spirit can do much more for the God seeker. Sat Guru can purify and unite.

In an instant, The Holy Spirit can transform the beliefs, thoughts, and wants of a person. This includes the neural pathways that facilitate them. The Spirit of God has the ability to bring a change to the body and mind, and that change is in harmony with the expectations of The Holy Spirit. After which, there is no need to struggle to control the body's influences because they no longer speak.

> *"But the fruit of the Spirit is love, joy, peace, patience, kindness, goodness, faithfulness."* — (Galatians 5:22)

If blessed, God's Spirit will gift The Word, and this sacred vibration has two general states, dormant and awake. In a person, when the resonance is awake, a type of rebirth occurs. The material nature is subdued by the nature of the spirit, and the place thoughts and actions are deliberated is lifted above the influences of the body and Maya/Mammon, the material illusion, to become a conduit for God's Will.

> *"He saved us, not because of righteous things we had done, but because of his mercy. He saved us through the washing of rebirth and renewal by the Holy Spirit."* — (Titus 3:5)

> *"Being born again, not of corruptible seed, but of incorruptible, by the word of God, which liveth and abideth forever."* — (1 Peter 1:23)

The Spirit of God has the power to set right the manner in which a person operates and a purification is a requirement before an individual can unite with The Formless. Consider this. The person is like a drop of water dyed with purple color, in a body of the clearest water. Until the purple color is removed from the droplet, it will never truly merge with the whole. Sat Guru eliminates that color. Without God's Spirit, regardless of how thin the color might get, the person will never truly merge.

God Unmanifest introduces God Spiritually-Manifest to the person, and the second unites the individual with God Unmanifest—God introduces the person to God. That is, after a rebirth. When a person is lifted, in full awareness, and as a member of the audience, an individual walks in God's Will and see God's play in action—as opposed to a player unaware of the play and trapped to the script.

An individual may have mastered their chakras, learned how to manipulate the principles of the Universe so to perform miracles, or accumulated all the wealth the planet has to offer, but without The Holy Spirit, a person will never know the true essence of ONE.

> *"Flesh gives birth to flesh, but the Spirit gives birth to spirit. You should not be surprised at my saying, 'You must be born again.' The wind blows wherever it pleases. You hear its sound, but you cannot tell where it comes from or where it is going. So it is with everyone born of the Spirit."* — (John 3:6-8)

After spending many years examining religions, I was blessed with a revelation, the awareness of God's Spirit. This doesn't mean the Holy Ghost appeared to me or anything of that sort. I was blessed with an intellectual awareness and I do not claim to know the entirety of The Holy Spirit's nature, or for that matter, the entirety of The Word's and the Christ's. I can't even claim to know the smallest percentile. I'm a mere mortal. The mysteries of God's Spirit only The Father knows. I only share the smallest portion of the shadow cast by the tiniest grain from the beach that is The All. I am a simple person like you. I do not claim prophetic powers, a celestial title, a mission from Heaven, or angelic communications. I am a simple person searching for The Father. Forgive me if I present myself otherwise.

"He was in the beginning with God. All things were made by him; and without him was not any thing made that was made. In him was life; and the life was the light of men. And the light shineth in darkness; and the darkness comprehended it not." — (John 1:2-5)

"He was in the world, and the world was made through Him, and the world did not know Him. He came to His own, and His own did not receive Him. But as many as received Him, to them He gave the right to become children of God..." — (John 1:10-12)

The popular interpretation of the above passages is that Jesus is the "he" and "him". Yet, this isn't what's written. "He" and "him" doesn't necessarily reference Jesus. I believe the terms personify God's Spirit or God's Word—leaning more toward the latter. It makes sense, especially after understanding the nature of God's Word as a sacred vibration and The Holy Ghost as The Great Architect.

Many men, who understood the power of the Word, stepped onto the battlefield. With all their faith in the Word, they felt invincible. They knew that the power of the Word deflects all bullets and arrows. They knew that the power of the Word seals all wounds before they occur. Unlock the Word, and you too can take your place amid heroes.

"As long as the mortal does not come to understand the mystery of the Shabad, the Word of God, he shall continue to be tormented by death." — (Sri Guru Granth Sahib Ji, ang 1126 of 1430)

I Salute The Spirit

> *"... the Spirit helps us in our weakness. We do not know what we ought to pray for, but the Spirit himself intercedes for us..."* — (Romans 8:26)

The person comes into the world innocent, with little knowledge of the reality cast into, and an individual learns of the world from the givers of information such as governments, movies, music, corporations, the family tree, and religions.

Regrettably, all of them have the potential to, purposely or accidentally, communicate inaccurate knowledge and a person can grow to live a life governed by an untruthful value system.

The consciousness can be misinformed and an individual can live a lie without knowing it. All the same, there is a teacher forever truthful and who is eternally incorruptible. This giver of knowledge will never purposely or unknowingly mislead an individual. I forever salute The Holy Ghost.

> *"But the Advocate, the Holy Spirit, whom the Father will send in my name, will teach you all things and will remind you of everything I have said to you."* — (John 14:26)

Love God and love all God's creations. In God's Mercy, the Lord will send The Spirit. The Holy Ghost truthfully teaches and Sat Guru can activate The Word within. The Word's resonance allows the "I" to experience the absolute reality. Through the mind of a mystic, union with The Great Architect can be achieved. A permanent love, in the truest sense, can soak through to every gene and every inch of a person's being. Salvation can be yours, and the first step is to believe.

How God's Spirit Answers

Ask God's Spirit and you will receive an answer.

The distance between you and a direct answer depends on the cleanliness of your magnetic field. The cleaner and stronger a person's invisible presence, the more direct the answer.

A dirty and weak metaphysical presence welcomes indirect and obscure answers, and for an untrained mind, it will be difficult to identify this type of answer. The response might briefly flash before an individual, and in the form of a sentence, within a book. Or the answer might reveal itself through another person and the ideas he or she is sharing. Or the answer might be illustrated through the behaviour of birds. The list of indirect methods of delivering an answer is unending and God's Spirit can orchestrate any invisible and visible thing within the Universe to convey a reply.

Those individuals with a clean and strong invisible presence receive direct answers and the most direct answer manifests as an inner whisper. God's Spirit can speak to a person, and from within, a person will hear.

My friend, do your best to garnish and maintain a superior aura. If you can achieve this, anything you wish to know can be known, and it will be a matter of asking the right question.

God is More

Popular culture has trapped the mind to think of God inside a box. This limits a person's spiritual cognisance.

When a person hears the word "God", their mind naturally brings forth the images and the associations they absorbed to represent the idea of God. It's similar to what happens when a person hears the word "apple", and the phenomenon can limit a person's awareness and spiritual progress.

I do not have the cognitive capability to give a full description of God, or even the smallest of the most miniscule of accounts. Yet, since my mind requires some sort of definition, I've learned to think of The One as the Sikh doctrine depicts The Great Architect, as the Beginning, the End, Timeless, Formless, Fathomless, Limitless, Omnipotent, Omniscient, and The Primal Energy—everything known and unknown—is contained within and differentiations from. Such a description resonates with my soul. The others limit my understanding of The Great-Giver. I just can't confine "God" to an image of an old man, with a white beard, floating amid the clouds, constantly wrestling the devil, and daily administering punishment. Or a young man, with dusty-blonde hair, and blue eyes. Or for that matter, a God represented by a particular colour, form, or gender.

Any attribute that limits the power of The Creator isn't truthful. God is much more and the human mind isn't powerful enough to grasp The Unfathomable. By limiting The Father, concepts such as the Christ, The Word, and Jesus' Godhood are immensely difficult to grapple with.

Although I use different names such as God, The Father, The Great-Giver, and The Great Architect to denote ONE, please recognize that my intention isn't to limit ONE inside a box.

....

When there was nothing, there was ONE. When there is nothing, there will be ONE.

The Trinity Unveiled

Within the Celestial Triangle are four equal triangles and the center triangle represents God/The Source. From God stem the other three triangles and they represent the Trinity. The Trinity is Universal.

The Universality of the Trinity might not be apparent since each true religion has forgotten. In their amnesia, new or partial associations surfaced. With the older traditions, these interpretations arose soon after the Bronze Age ended, near 5000 years ago.

This era was ushered in by an epic world battle and catastrophic natural disasters. This left behind a planet in chaos. Knowledge was lost. Civilizations were forced to start over again and only partial understanding was retained. Before this epoch, the Trinity was popularly understood as I explain it.

The three points are God's Word, God's Name, and God's Spirit. They are the keys to all creation and these three must be experienced before a person can unite with The Great Architect and achieve the highest existence, in this life and the next.

In the Egyptian tradition, Osiris represents God's Name, Horus represents God's Word, and Isis represents God's Spirit.

In the Hindu/Vedic house, Shiv represents God's Name, Brahma represents God's Word, and Vishnu represents God's Spirit.

Within the Sikh doctrine, Sat Naam represents God's Name, Shabad represents God's Word, and Sat Guru represents God's Spirit.

The sacred book of the Mayan Quiches, *the Popol-vuh*, suggests that Tzakol, The Supreme Diety, has three aspects: Bitol (the maker), Alom (the engenderer), and Qaholom (he who gives being).

Zoroaster represented the Triad as fire, sun, and light.

The ancient Chinese too respected a Triune God. As suggested by the Hi-Tse, The Great Unit, or Y, is three and three are the Great Unit. Yet, the Great Unit has neither body or shape. Tao-Tse, in his book, Tao-te-King, writes of the Triad: *"That reason, Tao, produced one. That one produced two, that both produced three; and that three had produced all things."* (*Sacred Mysteries, Among the Mayas and the Quiches. 11, 500 Years Ago.* By Augustus Le Plongeon, 1886).

In the Christian doctrine, these three are represented by Father, Son, and Holy Spirit. The Father represents God's Name. The Son represents God's Word. The Holy Spirit represents God's Spirit. Although Christianity was birthed in this Yug, the early Christian adepts understood the Trinity as above, but because of the European dark ages and the many political incursions, the Celestial Triangle is now understood as something else.

In some houses, such as Egypt's, the three now solely represent Solar, Lunar, and Stellar worship. Yet, in ancient times, Horus, Osiris, and Isis carried a dual meaning. Along with the association to astronomical bodies and movements, the three also represented The Word, The Name, and The Spirit.

From the Christian tradition, we learn that the Trinity is One. From the Egyptian adepts, we learn that Isis and Osiris are required for The Word to be. From the Vedic house, we learn that the three are able to manifest and take physical form. From the Chinese house, we learn that the three produce all things. From the Sikh tradition, we learn that without the Trinity, the highest salvation cannot be experienced.

The Trinity, as I've presented it, in my humble opinion, is the secret of secrets taught by the early Bronze Age mystery schools. Of course, I can't be sure. Their teachings are secret and those who know the lessons keep them locked within. I'm guessing an oath of secrecy is involved and loyal they are to that cause.

In my case, I'm the son of an uneducated immigrant and first generation to a developed nation. I come from the fringes of society and I've gone unnoticed. I've knocked on the door, once or twice, but I must be invisible because society opened the entrance, looked through me, took a few steps outside, glanced left, glanced right, and went back in—closing the door as they did.

Don't feel sorry for me. It was a blessing. Independently learning has come with a gift. In my ignorance, I'm free to express what others deem secrets.

Several ancient philosophers also understood the Celestial Triangle. For example, Orpheus and Plato represented The Creator/The Demiurgos as Triple—the Three Kings. And the Athenian philosopher, Damascius, celebrated The Infinite as a Thrice Unknown Darkness. Yet, above the Three Kings is The Emperor, The Infinite, known as "Ra" to the Chaldeans. (*Sacred Mysteries, Among the Mayas and the Quiches. 11, 500 Years Ago.* By Augustus Le Plongeon, 1886).

In the Beginning...

In the Beginning, the heavenly darkness was, and The Spirit and The Name, together, repelled the dark. After the darkness retreated, what remained was a celestial watery essence. The Spirit then moved over the watery essence and initiated creation.

The most philosophical manuscript coveted by the ancient Egyptians was *the Primander*. This book relates a conversation between Thoth and Primander, the Supreme Intelligence. Of creation, Thoth communicates the following:

> *"I had then before my eyes a most prodigious spectacle. All things had resolved themselves into light. A marvellous, pleasing and seducing sight it was to contemplate. It filled me with delight. After a while a horrid shadow, which ended in oblique folds, and assumed a humid nature, agitated itself with terrific noise. From it escaped smoke with uproar, and a voice was heard above the din. It seemed as the voice of the light; and the verb came forth from that voice of light; that verb was carried upon the humid principle. Out of it came forth the fire pure and light, and rising, it was lost in the air that, spirit-like, occupies the intermediate space between the water and the fire. The earth and the water were so mixed that the surface of the Earth covered by the water appeared nowhere." (Sacred Mysteries, Among the Mayas and the Quiches. 11, 500 Years Ago.* By Augustus Le Plongeon, 1886).

The sacred book of the Quiches, *Popol-Vuh*, conveys the following:

> *"This is the recital of how everything was without life, calm and silent, all was motionless and quiet; void was the immensity of the heavens; the face of the Earth did not manifest itself yet; only the tranquil sea was, and the space of*

the heavens. All was immobility and silence in the darkness..." (*Sacred Mysteries, Among the Mayas and the Quiches. 11, 500 Years Ago.* By Augustus Le Plongeon, 1886).

The Manava-dharma-sastra, a Vedic manuscript, suggests that:

"the visible universe in the beginning was nothing but darkness. Then the great, self-existing Power dispelled that darkness, and appeared in all His splendor. He first produced the waters; and on them moved Narayana *the divine spirit."* (*Sacred Mysteries, Among the Mayas and the Quiches. 11, 500 Years Ago.* By Augustus Le Plongeon, 1886).

The New Testament too contains a similar story.

"In the beginning the Earth was without form and void; and darkness was upon the face of the deep, and the spirit of God moved upon the face of the water. And God said, Let there be light and there was light." (*Sacred Mysteries, Among the Mayas and the Quiches. 11, 500 Years Ago.* By Augustus Le Plongeon, 1886).

The story of Isis, Osiris, and Set suggests that The Spirit and The Name together repel the heavenly darkness (Set). The story also implies that when The Spirit and The Name retract, Set will again reign.

The Beautiful and the Ugly

The mind suffers from duality. It's a natural happening. The two types of cognitive conditions a person accommodates are the beautiful and the ugly. Each condition is constituted by different beliefs and different cognitive units (cognitive units eventually mediated by a person's value system).

The Beautiful Cognitive Condition

The beautiful cognitive condition, also known as "the collective cognitive condition" and "the angelic half", develops, houses, nurtures and reinforces a value system constituted by such beliefs and wants as the following: contentment, compassion, truth, unconditional love, humility, virtue, righteousness, empathy, self-actualization, a transitive conscious condition, rationality, emotional stability, a desire for knowledge, the soul ("The Light Within"), a spiritual life purpose (a life purpose before and beyond a secular purpose), a sense of oneness with humanity, and a collective ego.

Collective ego
The ego represents the belief of the self, and although the substance of the ego is learned, the shell that houses this substance is innate. What's more, the ego is the captain of both cognitive conditions and a person will grow to develop either a dominant collective ego or a dominant selfish ego. The beliefs mentioned in the previous paragraph constitute the collective ego.

The Ugly Cognitive Condition

To describe the ugly half of the mind's dichotomy, the phrases "the selfish cognitive condition" and "the demonic half" are also used. The dominant characteristics of a selfish cognitive condition are those that:

1) Suppress, weaken, contradict, or disguise the elements of the angelic half.

2) Nurture only sensual fulfilment, a selfish existence, sensory satisfaction, individuality, and self-interest.

3) Separate the self from humanity, communities, other people, The Absolute, the spirit, the Universe, and the planet.

4) Detail the individual with a higher value than humanity, other people, communities, death, The Absolute, the spirit, the Universe, and the planet.

5) Nurture the selfish ego and the destructive elements. The destructive elements validate the existence of the selfish ego.

Selfish ego
The beliefs mentioned above constitute the selfish ego. In addition, the four destructive elements heavily influence the selfish ego. The four destructive elements within the mind are anger, lust, attachment, and greed. The destructive agents are so for several reasons: 1) They intensify the alienation of the mind from the collective cognitive condition and the behaviour and thoughts it generates. 2) They give rise for a person to hurt another. 3) They build and reinforce thoughts that strengthen the domination of a selfish cognitive condition. 4) And they have a nasty habit of destroying the person from within while alienating the mind from spiritual intention.

Anger is an innate emotional unit of the mind, and when it predominantly influences the mind, the mind turns onto the self. This state of perception limits the information a person uses in the decision-making process—the connections to the prefrontal cortex are blocked.

Lust is an innate ability of the mind, and it represents an intense and irrational want. Under the inductions of lust, the mind morphs into an island and is unable to construct thoughts outside the irrational want.

Attachment is an innate ability of the mind, and the term represents a mind unable to let go of a particular external or internal stimulation (memory, belief or want). An attachment results in the narrowing of a person's awareness, and detachment from the stimulant will typically cause the mind and body extreme pain and suffering.

Greed is a constructed want, and it represents an irrational and unmastered appetite. The term is applicable to the senses as much as it is to an irrational appetite for material objects, and as the other destructive elements, greed alienates the mind from the power of the collective cognitive condition and all that follows.

The agents of the selfish and the agents of the collective are doorways to the entire condition. When an element of a cognitive condition, such as anger, is dominantly influencing the place where thoughts are determined, that component will entice other elements of the selfish into a state of preparedness. Each aspect of a condition is linked to the other elements of that condition.

When either condition is dominant, the many other beliefs and wants an individual constructs will be framed by the foremost condition. Likewise, the other cognitive units with the potential to motivate motion, and the type of information an individual seeks, will be guided by the dominant condition.

Interestingly, the elements of each condition complement each other, and the elements of each cognitive condition also contradict the elements of the other. It would seem that they naturally fall into two camps, and because of this happening, to neglect the agents of the collective is to nurture the selfish, and to neglect the elements of the demonic is to nurture the angelic.

For the most part, a person volleys between the two conditions. However, a person will naturally grow to dominantly function through one of the two conditions—the half most strengthened and stimulated. Of the two, all the popular religions agree that the angelic has greater importance.

First and foremost, the selfish condition produces a state of being that isn't aligned to Heaven—the resonance it produces denies a celestial experience and pollutes a person's aura (magnetic field). The beautiful or the selfish, no matter what condition is the keeper of the consciousness, an emanation is generated and thoughts and actions are imprinted on it.

The aura of a person influences the experiences a person will attract. Like pulls like. Negative thoughts and feelings only bring about negative experiences. Thoughts, words, feelings, and actions created by the selfish condition also damage an individual's magnetic field and introduce suffering. The selfish not only facilitates suffering, it also recognizes and validates the suffering.

The beautiful condition, on the other hand, cleanses and strengthens a person's magnetic field. A clean and strong magnetic field is a must-have, before a person can experience Heaven on Earth. What's more, a strong field improves experiences, vitality, and health—mental, physical, and spiritual.

Secondly, all thoughts have invisible consequences, as demonstrated by Emoto's *Water Experiment,* and the thoughts and feelings produced by the beautiful do not produce a chaotic presence. However, the thoughts and feelings generated by the ugly half of the mind do. A chaotic presence denies spiritual progression and erects a barrier between the person and God's Spirit. Without God's Spirit, the Word will not be experienced, and without the Word, liberation is unattainable.

Thirdly, the angelic half of the mind allows the soul to speak, whereas the demonic half blocks the communications of this invisible component.

For the sake of convenience, I've decided to call the place where thoughts are projected, Thought Energy. Thought Energy is the "I" in this reality and the arena where we consciously dream, imagine, anticipate, build, converse, question, want, perceive, see, taste, smell, hear, think, feel, judge, plan, infer, administer, and evaluate. All conscious thoughts and actions are mapped there. When creating, perceiving, imagining, etc., Thought Energy is receiving and/or accessing information—no matter how insignificant and off the radar. The two sources from which information is sent or accessed through are the soul and the mind. (The mind is fixed to the brain and the brain is tied to the body). Thought Energy, in most cases, is initially more so influenced by the information and operations of the soul. However, the influence of the soul can grow to become a secondary source, or silent. This occurs when the mind evolves to understand itself as the lone source of information able to communicate to Thought Energy—a consequence of a dominant selfish cognitive condition. For some reason, the selfish naturally blocks the influences of the soul, whereas, the beautiful naturally allows the soul's influences to flow to Thought Energy.

Fourthly, the selfish cognitive condition can become a demonic possession and it can blind the "I" to spiritual life purposes. Under its influence, an individual's thoughts rarely travel further than the individual they inhibit—recognition and validation of the metaphysical diminishes. Under its influence, a person's perception of the self and other people becomes different, different compared to an empathetic or compassionate state of consciousness.

All the wrong that a person is capable of such as lying, cheating, stealing, adultery, promiscuity, bullying, injuring another, murder, exploitation, slander, and greed originate from the selfish half of the mind. Fiendishly, the ugly blurs the influence of the beautiful as the smog that hides the shine of the stars at night.

The same is true when the beautiful is the mind's lord, but in the opposite sense, and the angelic hides the darkness by emanating light. When the beautiful is the dominant condition, ugly thoughts remain just that and demonic thoughts rarely enter the thought process. If they do, the influences of the beautiful are typically able to suppress them.

Finally, the selfish condition restricts a person's ability to meditate and properly pray—with all the mind's focus. That by harassing Thought Energy as an individual is attempting to silence and direct the mind. The beautiful condition doesn't have the same distracting effect. Without meditating and travelling through the self, the fruit of salvation will not be tasted. Without the fruit, even though the body is breathing, the mind is dead.

"For to be carnally minded is death, but to be spiritually minded is life and peace." — (Romans 8:6)

The beautiful is the better of the two conditions and it cocoons the ideal state of mind—an awareness conducive to spiritual progress. But unfortunately, the entire world loves the selfish cognitive condition more than the beautiful. It's been like this since the time of Jesus. A God seeker must be vigilant if to survive worldly influences.

Eventually, if a person is able to master their ugly half, and if they wish to continue the spiritual journey, he or she will need to overpower the beautiful half too. Both conditions are of the body, and for the spirit to fully communicate and influence Thought Energy unobstructed, all the body's influences must be silenced. This, however, cannot happen without celestial assistance. But worry not, if a person is genuinely progressing, The Father will help. God is kind.

"Knowing others is wisdom, knowing yourself is Enlightenment." — Lao Tzu

Lost in Translation

Many don't know this but Jesus never wrote what he thought or preached. Words were attributed to him decades after he ascended into "The White Light". Men other then he wrote *the Gospels* and each writer plausibly mixed in his own personality.

Clear evidence of this is the disagreements and the contradictions between the different adaptations of *the Bible*, such as those between *the New International* version and *the King James* version—supposedly edited by Francis Bacon. For example, the following passage, in *the New International* version, suggests everything is predetermined and predestined, and the same passage, in *the King James* version, suggests a person reaps what he or she sows.

> *"Whoever has ears, let them hear. 'If anyone is to go into captivity, into captivity they will go. If anyone is to be killed with the sword, with the sword they will be killed.'"* — (Revelation 13:9-10, New International Version)

> *"If any man have an ear, let him hear. 'He that leadeth into captivity shall go into captivity: he that killeth with the sword must be killed with the sword.'"* — (Revelation 13:9-10, King James Version)

Surprisingly, there are over 100 different editions of *the Bible* and each is slightly different.

Further confirmation of the mix is the inconsistencies between the authors of *the Gospels*.

> *"Mark says that Jesus was crucified the day after the Passover meal was eaten (Mark 14:12; 15:25) and John says he died the day before it was eaten (John 19:14)... Luke indicates in his account of Jesus's birth that Joseph and Mary returned to*

Nazareth just over a month after they had come to Bethlehem and performed the rites of purification (Luke 2:39), whereas Mathew indicates they instead fled to Egypt (Matt. 2:19-22)."¹

Even though names are given, there is no method to confirm who actually wrote *the New Testament*,² and author Jack Nelson-Pallmeyer, in his book, *Is Religion Killing Us?: Violence in the Bible and the Quran* (2005), makes an interesting observation about one of the supposed, Mathew.

"Matthew is often an unreliable witness of Jesus. In his parables Jesus repeatedly exposes key actors in the oppressive system, only to have Matthew present those exposed as 'God figures' that Matthew blesses with the authority of Jesus' voice. These 'God figures' consistently send people to the torturers or to other terrible punishments."

In all fairness, it's very possible that the authors of *the Gospels* were guided by a Divine Will. Thus, making their words the Words of God, but the originals are lost, and over the centuries, words were changed, translated, dropped, or added. What we have today is not what originally was. Maybe, that's why contradictions exist. Perhaps, that why so many Divine notions, such as God's Word and the Christ, aren't properly explained. Author John Vaughan asserts:

"...the original writers were preserved from all error by the direct assistance of the Holy Ghost, this Divine assistance does not extend to the individual monks or friars, or other scribes, however holy, who sat down, pen in hand, to reproduce the original text."³

Furthermore, *the Gospels* were initially communicated orally⁴ and when the practice of recording them in writing came to be, unintentional and intentional errors were made.

"...scribes occasionally altered the words of their sacred texts to make them more patently orthodox."[5]

"At times scribes would make intentional changes as they copied. For example, they would correct what they believed to be a spelling error in their source text. And even the best of scribes also sometimes made unintended errors."[6]

"There were thousands and thousands of copyists busily employed in the monasteries and scriptoriums through the world. Through want of observation or through carelessness or weariness, or on account of difficult or partially effaced writing, how easy it was to mistake a letter, or to omit a word or a particle; yet such an omission is capable of altogether changing the sense of an entire passage. The accidental dropping of even a single letter may sometimes make a striking difference."[7]

"Attestations of variants within the lectionary tradition are so manifold that there is little plausibility in the theory that at the beginning of the lectionary tradition there was one specific text set up for liturgical reading that was then copied as a unity and in the course of its history increasingly brought into agreement with the mainstream. It appears to be more likely that different text forms fed into the lectionary tradition and were carefully copied and 'commonly and officially used.'"[8]

In relation, the contemporary English *Gospels* are all translations of translations of translations.[9] The original *Gospels* didn't survive. What we have are translations of copies of the originals and not translations of the originals (autographs).[10] Bart Ehrman, an expert on the topic, writes:

"So rather than actually having the inspired words of the autographs (i.e., the originals) of the Bible, what we have are the error-ridden copies of the autographs."[11]

> *"We have only error-ridden copies, and the vast majority of these are centuries removed from the originals and different from them, evidently, in thousands of ways."*[12]

> *"What good does it do to say that the words are inspired by God if most people have absolutely no access to these words, but only to more or less clumsy renderings of these words into a language, such as English, that has nothing to do with the original words?"*[13]

Three centuries after the death of Jesus, under the guidance of Emperor Constantine, an extremely powerful politician, who supposedly saw a cross in the sky before a decisive battle, the Christian doctrine was solidified. But during the process, not all of *the Gospels* were included and knowledge was purposely hidden.[14] And debated doctrine such as—was Jesus God, the Son of God, or a mortal man—were arbitrarily put to rest by one person who was allegedly considered a heretic by the Christians,[15] and who's been repeatedly proven inaccurate by contemporary historians, Eusebius, the Emperor's religious advisor.[16] It's a fact that before Constantine consolidated the Christian doctrine, *"thousands of documents existed chronicling His life (Jesus' life) as a mortal man."*[17]

So, why would an emperor prefer to ally himself with God, or the Son of God, and not a mortal man? The answer is simple. God and the Son are more powerful than any man is. It's always more advantageous to ally with the more powerful.

Not only was the above doctrine challenged, many Christians also questioned dogma like that presented in *Apocalypse (Book of Revelation)*. They considered it sacrilegious.[18] That is, taken at face value. *Apocalypse*, when decoded, is actually a journey through the self.

Now, why would Constantine allow such literature as part of the Christian doctrine? Divine punishment is required to keep the people obedient and dependent on the institution providing the means to salvation from that divine punishment. *Apocalypse* provides very descriptive images of that divine punishment. Those images create vivid pictures within the mind. This experience reinforces the overall idea of a divine punishment. Also, as every good emperor knows, the people must be willing to act violently to maintain and expand an empire. The violence within *Apocalypse* desensitizes a person to violence and contributes to this end.

It should be noted that before Constantine decided to embrace Christendom, the Christians were persecuted by the Roman Empire and their sacred books were destroyed. Not all of the recorded truths of Jesus and Christianity were available when Constantine decided to consolidate the Christian faith.[19]

During the melding process, there were Christians who didn't agree with Constantine's version of Christianity. However, they didn't object because they feared that the Emperor would punish them. Two actually did disagree and they were exiled.[20]

After Constantine's interference, what is now the Catholic Church remained, the other Christian groups were vilified and persecuted,[21] and all competing *Gospels* were destroyed.[22]

Before Constantine, the different Christian perspectives debated but they rarely resorted to violence. Even though some people propagated horrid opinions.[23]

> *"Blessed are the peacemakers, for they shall be called sons of God."* — (Matthew 5:9)

But after Constantine, violence was used to consolidate *the New Testament* and the power of those who held it. This is something I think Jesus would probably disagree with. He believed in peace and not violence as the instrument best equipped to reveal God's Kingdom.

The unification of Christianity further included the conversion of the Catholic clergy into employees of Rome.[24] The clergy adopted the titles of the Roman Government and changed in demeanour to reflect their Roman status.[25] As you can guess, after the Romans gave importance to the Church, the Church started attracting power and wealth. Subsequently, *"power-hungry, greedy politicians began to take over positions of leadership"*.[26]

Author David L. Dungan astutely recaps Constantine's interference in his book, *Constantine's Bible: politics and the making of the New Testament* (Fortress Press: Philadelphia, 2006).

> *"...the newly Christian emperor's efforts to influence virtually every aspect of his newfound ally, Catholic Christianity—from building new churches to paying clergy out of the state treasury, to intervening in church disputes, to convening councils of bishops and issuing edicts and making their decisions the law of the realm, to helping to determine the date for celebrating Easter to mandating Sunday as the universal day of worship, to outlawing heresy, to de facto implementations of Eusebius's 'acknowledged books' as the standard Bible of the Catholic Church."* — (Page 94-95)

Although the Church suggests that *the Gospels* are contamination free, this isn't the case. Nevertheless, *the Gospels* are still valuable and they're precious in the sense that they communicate important lessons and messages—more so if a person is able to decode the symbols and hidden meanings. I was born and raised amid the Christians and the true Christian is a person of excellent character. But to say that *the New Testament* is uncorrupted and completely accurate isn't truthful.

Lost in Translation: Endnotes

1. Bart D. Ehrman, Whose Words Is it? The story behind who changed the New Testament and Why (Continuum International Publishing Group LTD: New York, 2008), p. 10.

2. Translated by George Eliot, The Life of Jesus: critically examined (C. Blanchard, 1860), p. 41-54.

3. John S. Vaughan, Concerning the Holy Bible: Its use and abuse (Benziger Bros: New York, 1904), p. 11-12.

4. Peter Stravinskas, The Catholic Church and the Bible (Ignatius Press: San Francisco, 1996), p. 17.

5. Bart D. Ehrman, The Orthodox Corruption of Scripture: the effect of early Christological controversies in the text of the New Testament (Oxford University Press: USA, 1996), p. xi.

6. Mark D. Roberts, Can We Trust the Gospels? investigating the reliability of Mathew, Mark, Luke, and John (Good News Publishers: Illinois, 2007), p. 27.

7. John S. Vaughan, Concerning the Holy Bible: Its use and abuse (Benziger Bros: New York, 1904), p. 12.

8. DC Parker and Jeff Childers, Transmission and Reception: New Testament text-critical and exegetical studies (Gorgias Press: New Jersey, 2006), p. 40.

9. Mark D. Roberts, Can We Trust the Gospels?: investigating the reliability of Mathew, Mark, Luke, and John (Good News Publishers: Illinois, 2007), p. 28.

10. John S. Vaughan, Concerning the Holy Bible: Its use and abuse (Benziger Bros: New York, 1904), p. 14.

11. Bart D. Ehrman, <u>Misquoting Jesus; the story behind who changed the Bible and why</u> (Harper San Francisco: San Francisco, 2007), p. 5.

12. Bart D. Ehrman, <u>Whose Words Is it? The story behind who changed the New Testament and Why</u> (Harper San Francisco: San Francisco, 2005), p.7.

13. Ibid.

14. Bart D. Ehrman, <u>Lost Scriptures: books that did not make it into the New Testament</u> (Oxford University Press: Oxford; New York, 2003).

15. Christians Timothy David Barnes, <u>Constantine and Eusebius</u> (Harvard University Press: Massachusetts, 1981), p. 216.

16. David L. Dungan, <u>Constantine's Bible: politics and the making of the New Testament</u> (Fortress Press: Philadelphia, 2006), pg 112.

17. Bart D. Ehrman, <u>Truth and Fiction in the Da Vinci Code: a historian reveals what we really know about Jesus, Mary Magdalene, and Constantine</u> (Oxford University: New York, 2004), p. 98.

18. Alexander Campbell and John Baptist Purcell, <u>A Debate on the Roman Catholic Religion: held in Sycamore Street Meeting House</u>, Cincinnati, from the 13th to the 21st of January, 1837 (J.A. James, 1837), p. 55.

19. Max Arthur Macauliffe, <u>The Sikh Religion, Volume 1</u> (Forgotten Books, 2008), p. 60. [http://www.google.com/books?id=E0UwOOjrjGAC&dq=The+Sikh+Religion]

20. David L. Dungan, <u>Constantine's Bible: politics and the making of the New Testament</u> (Fortress Press: Philadelphia, 2006), p. 112.

21. Ibid., p. 109.

22. Ibid., p. 116.

23. William Anderson Scott, <u>The Bible and Politic: or, An humble plea for equal, perfect, absolute religious freedom, and against all sectarianism in our public schools</u> (H.H. Bancroft, 1859), p. 83.

24. David L. Dungan, <u>Constantine's Bible: politics and the making of the New Testament</u> (Fortress Press: Philadelphia, 2006), p. 102.

25. Ibid., p. 96.

26. Ibid., p. 125.

Dialogue and Plot

If the dialogue and the plot in a Holy Book advocate war, senseless terror, fear to gain obedience, murder, persecution, divisions, irrational conclusions, oppression, denial of other true religions, and thieving motivations, the dialogue and plot were probably altered to motivate people to behave in a specific manner, and to help them view reality through a particular set of eyeglasses. Alterations to this effect stem from a political, personal, or economic agenda. Religious corruption is further explored in the book, *War and Religion.*

....

God is strictly benevolent—God loves all creation. If a religion promotes the opposite, rest assured that the religion is coveting nonsense. But this doesn't mean religion doesn't shelter a God awareness. With an openness to selfish and ungodly intentions, study the spiritual path, the stories, the history, and the literature religion gives. Interpreted correctly, they are food for the soul and they will take you closer to the angelic.

Serpents, Doves, and Tricksters

All true religions are under attack, including Christianity, and already, the battle has played through many, many centuries.

To add to the suspense, each person is born without knowledge of the war and each person is born trusting the givers of information such as pastors and preachers. However, those entrusted to guide the flock sometimes misdirect the God seeker. They do so because they were misdirected by their teachers.

The high-level religious instructors, the teachers of the common pastor and preacher, are misteaching some notions. The root of the tree is polluted. The low-level religious teachers—the pastors and preachers, afraid to question their instructors, are unaware of the contamination, and unintentionally, they teach those who come to them the same misdirection. The low-level teachers are typically good people who want to help others. It's not their intentions I question but the knowledge they were taught by those higher-up the ladder than them. Too many low-level teachers are actually students pretending to be masters.

Don't get me wrong, not all Christian institutions, designated to train pastors or preachers, are intentionally or unintentionally misleading their students. I'm sure there's a place of learning, somewhere, that isn't infected.

Be vigilant when the itch to learn more about God and the spiritual kingdom surfaces. Most individuals will naturally walk through the doors of a church, mosque, synagogue, gurudawara, temple, ashram, etc. looking for answers. However, that probably isn't the best place to begin the search for truth.

Religious institutions such as churches are great places to meditate on The Father, but not the ideal places to learn about The Source and the spiritual kingdom. A person might be misdirected. The spiritual path might be missed and replaced with a counterfeit.

Self-study is one of the more viable options. A person has a better chance of gaining higher understanding by reading the different Holy Books and spiritual books without the interference of low-level teachers. After which, walk through the doors of whatever religion compels you and continue your learning. All the while, beg The Holy Ghost to conduct a lecture. Love The Ultimate Teacher.

Fool's Gold

Many believers rely on the interpretations of *the Gospels* to understand Jesus, instead of reading *the Gospels*. I guess the length of *the New Testament* can be a little intimidating and it's easier to read or listen to a summary. Yet, the danger is in the interpretation. Some are purposely misleading and others unintentionally misdirect—regardless the interpretation's popularity. Through the popular, too often, fools are made of men and women.

False literature and supposed ancient texts are also created and propagated to misdirect the truth seeker. It's as if there's a thick layer of dirt masking truthful spiritual knowledge, and if a person doesn't recognize it, he or she is certain to be soiled.

Oh, and it doesn't end there. According to Myron Fagan, an American writer/producer/director, in a lecture conducted several decades back, a religion-orientated institution is occasionally established for the purpose of creating confusion and propagating false information as accurate. The ruling classes are all too familiar with the tools of deception.

An Enemy or a Friend?

Reason is not an enemy. Reason is a gift from The Father and given to every person so to determine what is Godly and what is not.

Those churches that characterize "reason" as an evil are cunning creatures. Without the God given tool that is "reason" filtering the information absorbed by the mind and the body, these churches can teach any fantastical version of Christianity they desire, without opposition. Lies can be sold as truth and Heaven might not be the end destination.

Reason is not an enemy. Reason is a trusted companion—a best of friends able to guide a person past the falsehoods and to The Light. Those who teach that reason is a foe might be harbouring a hidden agenda, or they only repeat what the higher-ups are telling them. Whatever it is, reason is a God given tool, and the more knowledge a person feeds it, the more able it is to reason the existence of The Great Eternal.

Jesus vs. Jesus

The Cross and Jesus

Before I better understood the image of dead Jesus on a cross, the depiction provoked uncomfortable feelings. The symbol shows the superhuman Jesus as a defeated person. But how can this be when Jesus was under the protection of God? Nothing can penetrate The Father's Shield.

The mainstream interpretation didn't do much to quell my discomfort. If anything, it spawned more confusion. Serendipitously, I stumbled across a very old understanding. According to Manly P. Hall, the ancient adepts of the world symbolized Maya/Mammon, or the material, as a cube. An unfolded cube takes the shape of a cross.

Along this line of thought, Jesus' dead body on the cross represents the triumph of the spirit over the human body and Maya (this includes both the cognitive conditions). It's the death of the material body while still living, the resurrection of the spirit, and Jesus' rebirth through it. As mentioned, this occurs by way of God's Word, and after a resurrection, the subconscious merges with an individual's conscious state and the principle element influencing this awareness is the spirit, and the commander of the spirit is The Father.

The image further depicts a fragile Jesus. This teaches us that spiritual growth includes immense suffering. Without suffering, and for an ego-centered mind, typically, the consciousness will not expand to seek and comprehend more than Mammon. Suffering breaks the egoic bubble and swells a person's awareness to validate the spiritual and the spirit. Suffering is a blessing.

The egoic bubble evolves as a person, under the dominance of the ego, interacts with the material world, and the bubble's value system is centered on the supremacy of the egoic self and Mammon. This bubble limits a person's awareness of reality—without an individual knowing it.

Suffering bursts the bubble, and unfortunately, this will likely bring about more suffering. Cognitive dissonance and depression is a natural outcome when a value system no longer holds prominence or worth. A person who then interacts with society and her members, under the influence of a shattered value system, will surely and slowly experience social and financial marginalization. The most painful side-effect will be friends and family who do not understand. The isolation and ridicule will hurt. Resource less to purchase help, many nights will be spent crying out to the Universe.

Loneliness, ridicule, and poverty, accompanied by cognitive dissonance and depression, can provoke suicidal thoughts and many dances with the shadow of Death. But hopefully, the individual experiencing the aftermath of the burst is strong enough to endure this trial by fire, and through the suffering, able to sweep away the ashes and construct a more truthful value system— one no longer centered on the egoic self and Maya.

Suffering can rupture the egoic bubble and this is the first step to conquering the body's influences and recognizing reality before and beyond the material. Suffering is a prerequisite to sainthood.

The ego is the Captain of the body, and if it can be captured, as can the army (the body's influences such as anger and greed). But once it's taken into custody, the ego and its army will torment the warden (the person attempting to evolve past the body). This too causes extreme agony. Yet, if a person can keep them imprisoned long enough, with meditation, proper thought, proper conduct, and prayer, God's Spirit will descend and permanently switch off the influences of the body—The Holy Ghost will permanently quiet the captors.

To live for more than the material and to master the body involves immense suffering. No person can truly empathize with those who've survived the fire. Only those who've also experienced the flames can. People as Jesus deserve their status. They are kings amid men and women.

In my interpretation, the symbol of dead Jesus on a cross has evolved to host a dual meaning. In this, the initial understanding represents so much more than the popular depiction. Nor does it show Jesus as a defeated person. On the contrary, Jesus is depicted as superhuman, for Jesus conquered Mammon and transformed into a Christ. The cross is a symbol of Jesus' Christhood.

Since we're discussing the symbol of the cross, the cross is not exclusive to Christendom and the symbol was used for many, many millennia before the birth of Jesus. Nor is the cross a universal symbol representing one particular notion. Sometimes, it denotes the Sun. Sometimes, it represents east, west, north, and south. Sometimes, it symbolizes the number 9. Sometimes, when with a circle, it's an astrological tool. Sometimes, it symbolizes the water deities. Sometimes, it's an emblem of heaven and immortality. And sometimes, it's associated to the Christ.

If the interpretation I present is correct, how is it that Jesus on the cross is understood differently?

Christendom experienced the European dark ages and it's possible the people of then didn't understand the cross as symbolic. To explain the image, they invented the story of the crucifixion. To add, Jewish literature suggests that the Magnificent Jesus was hung, along with five of his disciples, and they do not mention a crucifixion (*Babylonian Sanhedrin,* 43a-b). Perhaps, this is a lie? Maybe, it's propaganda? Yet, it does correlate to this articles interpretation of the cross. Take it for what you will. I'm still on the fence with what circumstances surrounded Jesus' ascendance.

In all honesty, for me, how Jesus was martyred doesn't shake my faith in Christendom. May it be the cross, may it not. It's all good. I love Jesus and Jesus made the ultimate sacrifice. But one thing is certain. Jesus allowed them to murder his body. I am confident of this. A Christ doesn't fear death. A Christ knows his or her strength will significantly increase as a bodiless creation. His executioners only strengthened Jesus and his influence. Perhaps, that's why the Christians survived the wrath of the vicious Romans, for over three-hundred years. The bodiless Christ was their helper. His executioners only executed themselves. The Christ is incredible. A moment of remembrance is in order.

....

What is sometimes labelled an evil isn't actually dark. Labels are given to keep the truth seeker away from the truth. Manly P. Hall is one. A spiritual adept he was, yet, some churches call him a Devil worshipper. Manly P. Hall was a truth seeker. Read his words and judge for yourself.

Dead yet Alive

> *"Then Jesus said to His disciples, "If anyone desires to come after Me, let him deny himself, and take up his cross, and follow Me. For whoever desires to save his life will lose it, but whoever loses his life for My sake will find it. For what profit is it to a man if he gains the whole world, and loses his own soul? Or what will a man give in exchange for his soul?"* — (Matthew 16:24-26)

The Glorious Jesus taught his follows how to perform greater miracles than him, but this lesson is lost in translation and the truth of the matter is hidden. Luckily, the teaching can be decoded and the first step is to carry your own cross and to do as Jesus. Yet, to literally bare the cross will not gift a person salvation, and to carry the cross is to battle the body's influences and the material stimulants that love the body's programming more than the spirit's. To carry the cross is to slay one's physical presence without actually dying.

To kill the body while still alive is to dominate the body's programming/constitution, so to allow the spirit's constitution to influence the conscious framework. The body houses units of information such as anger and sadness. These units allow a person to experience such things as anger and sadness. Without these units of information, a person will not experience anger or sadness and Thought Energy is free of these influences. This is the goal, to be free of the body's programming. When this occurs, the spirit rises.

The spirit too houses units of information, along with tools equivalent to the body's senses—they allow the consciousness to sense what the five body senses cannot. The units of the spirit produce a conscious awareness different from a Thought Energy influenced by the body's units. It is an awareness aligned with The Father.

Only those who rise above the influences of their body and free the spirit will live right. But how many people can levitate above Mammon? The impulses of the body are strong. Daily, even the smartest, the strongest, the richest, and the most influential person is overpowered by them.

Many claim they've reached this state of awareness, and to be a born again Christian, in its truest definition, is to allow the spirit to rise above the body's influences. Yet, regardless of how many claim rebirth—as difficult as it might be to accept—only a few are truly reborn. True rebirth is much more laborious than the best-selling version. True rebirth is to capture the body and to allow the spirit to resurrect.

....

The Holy Spirit can assist a person conquer the body, but this doesn't guarantee Salo Ghost will gift the full power of The Word. Defeating the body doesn't guarantee the highest spiritual evolution.

Victory over Mammon doesn't ensure Christhood. There are different grades of being. The awakened state of The Word has different degrees. No matter, any category is superior to those trapped to the darkness of the body.

The Purpose of Suffering

Every other person believes their suffering has purpose. Yet, not many know this purpose. They know not because the knowledge of the self, in this epoch, is allusive.

After a person experiences extreme agony, the consciousness expands and opens to higher thoughts and information. This is the purpose of suffering, to expand the consciousness. However, if not embraced, and after prolonged peace, the consciousness will retract like an elastic band. This is sure to bring about more suffering. Until an expanded consciousness is recognized and clinched, extreme agony will keep coming again and again. It's a Universal absolute.

Silence isn't the body's desired disposition. It's contrary to its nature. The body loves to speak to Thought Energy as if it was the star of the show. But unlike a classy superstar, the body throws a temper tantrum when it doesn't land the lead role. To attempt to silence the body is to provoke the body even more.

The Pain of Jesus

> *"Then the soldiers of the governor took Jesus into the Praetorium and gathered the whole garrison around Him. And they stripped Him and put a scarlet robe on Him. When they had twisted a crown of thorns, they put it on His head, and a reed in His right hand. And they bowed the knee before Him and mocked Him, saying, 'Hail, King of the Jews!' Then they spat on Him, and took the reed and struck Him on the head. And when they had mocked Him, they took the robe off Him, put His own clothes on Him, and led Him away to be crucified."* —
> (Matthew 27:26-31)

The death of Jesus is depicted harshly. Is this to symbolize the cruelty and suffering a person will experience if they journey to conquer the influences of the body? Moreover, the cross represents the material realm. Is this why Jesus carries his own cross?

To conquer the self and the material world is to harbour a different set of beliefs, and rarely is family, property, career, and status entertained by the mind. Since most humans are caught in the net of a materialistic living and few individuals value the spiritual journey, most people will not understand the person attempting to defeat Mammon, and they will naturally ridicule, slander, and hate—even friends and family will participate—loneliness will be the only true mate.

The lack of faith in material means will also cause a lack of bread, clothing, and disposable money, and the body's unfulfilled needs will stimulate cognitive pain. The suffering is deep. The mind will transform into a temporary enemy.

It's an arduous task to carry the cross, and to journey to conquer the self is to stand against everything worldly. Yet, it doesn't end there. Unwittingly, the journey will naturally catch the attention of Darkness. Humanity is in utter

Darkness and the Darkness is permitted to govern. The unpersonified Devil, also known as Kal Yug, is the governor.

Humanity is in the Age of Darkness but do not think this epoch isn't sanction by The Great Architect. As difficult as it might be to comprehend, all is under the command of The Father, even the bad. Darkness is permitted to cause havoc. Darkness was crowned prince by The Maker.

> *"Then Jesus was led by the Spirit into the wilderness to be tempted by the devil."* — (Matthew 4:1)

The Darkness is a force of immense power and influence, but eventually, the crown is taken from Darkness, by The ONE who gave it. In the meantime, the saints, and those who journey to conquer the material, suffer through this era, while the remainder of humanity swims in blissful ignorance.

Darkness rules but the Light (spiritual truth) is not dead. The Light still lives. But a flicker from a flame it is, scattered and hidden.

Darkness can sense the vibrations of a consciousness in progression. Darkness is pulled by it. Those who seek the Light, those who journey to conquer the self, as Jesus did, are subject to Darkness's unneeded attention. It's Darkness's nature. Darkness must protect its sanctioned reign. Darkness must preserve its power and Darkness has no power over a person who's transcended the material. Moreover, those who live through the spirit are examples of a better living, and an example has the power to inspire others to do the same. Darkness must protect its rule and it does so by interfering with the seeker's search.

Darkness has many powers. Darkness has many methods. Darkness has many tricks. As scary as it is, everything that lives in Darkness is a potential vessel for the will of Darkness.

The initial interference will be slight, and if a person continues their journey toward Light, the interference will intensify. The end goal of Darkness is to redirect the seeker's thoughts and beliefs away from the Light.

The stimulation of anger, lust, attachment, pride, and greed are the most distracting. To this end, Darkness can directly influence a seeker's thoughts through whispers, and if this fails, Darkness will indirectly lay siege.

Darkness can distract the seeker's mind by pleasing the body's senses. Orchestrate it does events, people, and beliefs to this end—intensifying the illusionary rewards as a person's resistance gains momentum. Sometimes, kingship over the Earth is even offered—as Jesus experienced.

> *"And the devil, taking him up into an high mountain, shewed unto him all the kingdoms of the world in a moment of time. And the devil said unto him, All this power will I give thee, and the glory of them: for that is delivered unto me; and to whomsoever I will I give it. If thou therefore wilt worship me, all shall be thine."* — (Luke 4:5-7)

Darkness can distract the mind by pre-occupying it with useless life purposes, and unfortunately, each person is born innocent, to a world already in motion, and each develops their value configurations as they experience the matrix—*the second beast*.

And Darkness can disturb the mind by provoking the seeker's negative emotions. Since everything is a potential vessel, many times, other people are used as provocateurs—without their awareness. In my opinion, this type of attack can cause extreme suffering within the Light seeker, and lead to another happening.

When an individual is in a negative emotional state, their magnetic field weakens. This allows invisible predatory creatures to enter a person's sphere of existence. These creatures are attracted to negative emanations. It's a food source for them. They too require energy to exist. Unfortunately, a person can sometimes become their buffet. If a predator does enter, it will eventually provoke negative thoughts and behaviour to further generate negative emotions. The predator will perpetually distract the mind of the Light seeker until repelled.

Darkness has many methods, and those as Jesus, who aren't so easily distracted, experience the full wrath of Darkness. If a seeker can't be steered away by pleasure and false purposes, suffer they do immensely. Family, friends, and strangers will be used as puppets by Darkness. Everything that a person knows in this world might turn against the Light seeker, and their entire reality might shatter.

No one can understand the suffering of people as Jesus but another as Jesus. No one is able to empathize until he or she has experienced the full fury of Darkness.

Try and remember a moment in your life when you experienced deep suffering. Perhaps, it happened when a relationship with a lover ended, maybe, when a parent passed on, or perhaps, when you lost a significant material possession. Whatever it was that provoked the pain within, multiply it by many thousands and still you will not grasp the pain of Jesus.

I hope after reading this you'll love Jesus even more. Jesus made the ultimate sacrifice. Jesus sacrificed the body. But his sacrifice wasn't without immense suffering. To journey to conquer the self is to stand against everything worldly, and unwittingly, the journey will naturally catch the attention of Darkness.

The true saints are few, the true saints are marginalized, and the true saints bare the dull edge of the rusted sword that is the Iron Age. The dark-side, by the laws of the Universe, the laws of God, is permitted to ride on the righteous. The dark-side is sanctioned by The Great-Giver to do as it does.

Luckily, God has a plan. The true saints will emerge as the champions. The rule of Kal Yug is destined to end.

Misunderstood Genius

Jesus, the tanned-skinned genius, was misunderstood by almost all the people of his day. This caused near everyone to point, everyone to hate, everyone to misjudge, and everyone to slander. It must've felt as if the entirety of what Jesus knew hated him. The anguish he must've experienced.

Yet, Jesus did not conform. He believed in The Father and knew The Father as true. Nor did he retaliate against those who ridiculed his journey to Christhood. He controlled his body's outbursts. All the while, transcending it all and allowing his spirit to rise and be reborn.

My fellow God lover, Jesus is the best of us—he conquered inner pains we can't even begin to imagine. My brethren, we are weak compared to this tanned-skinned genius.

....

To understand the genius we now call Jesus, fathom his sorrow to apprehend his greatness.

The Missing Link

The highest teaching, just below The Source, is kept by every true religion. All the same, in the contemporary world, intentionally or unintentionally, it's concealed. The flock are not taught.

Perhaps, the religious teachers do not believe it possible. Maybe, the school or teacher they learnt under didn't teach them of it. Perhaps, its knowledge misunderstood many centuries ago, during the period before the Renaissance, and still requires corrective attention. Whatever it is, the art of mastering the body, so to allow the spirit to influence Thought Energy, isn't in the curriculum.

So, let me share with you a little more of the person who is a victor. Once a person has defeated Mammon/Maya, he or she will walk in the Will of God and they will perform miracles. Moreover, in such a state of existence, everything he or she does is correct. This is not to say such a person can commit an evil and this too is correct. In such a person, evil doesn't enter the time and space of thought, as it might in the mind of the non-adept. It's not even an option. Their being isn't capable of generating the required thoughts to commit an evil act. The units within him or her housing the information able to persuade a person's thoughts to conceive and justify evil thoughts aren't active, they're turned off.

Mike Bhangu

"The real meaning of enlightenment is to gaze with undimmed eyes on all darkness." — Niko Kazantzakis

The Dead and the Living

In the eyes of a spiritual adept, those who do not realize the spirit are as good as dead, while he or she still has breath. True living is living in God's Will.

True living cannot be experienced until the influences of the body are silenced and the spirit within is governing the time and space of thought. The path is narrow like the sharp edge of a sword. However, there is no other way if a person wishes to live truthfully. Until then, dead and in darkness a person is.

> *"Then they went in and did not find the body of the Lord Jesus. And it happened, as they were greatly[b] perplexed about this, that behold, two men stood by them in shining garments. Then, as they were afraid and bowed their faces to the earth, they said to them, 'Why do you seek the living among the dead? He is not here, but is risen!'"* — (Luke 24:3-6)

The New Testament speaks of two deaths and two resurrections.

> *"Blessed and holy is he that hath part in the first resurrection: on such the second death hath no power, but they shall be priests of God and of Christ, and shall reign with him a thousand years."* — (Revelation 20:6)

In my interpretation, after applying my spiritual understanding, the first death symbolizes the death of the body while a person still lives, and the second death is the release of the true self from the body. In the second death, the body is actually dead.

That individual who experiences the first death, in this life and after the body perishes, truly lives, and after the second death, they exist as God's favorites. But, if the first death isn't achieved, the second death will not be the highest manifestation.

If the first death is experienced, it's vital to stay the course. Jesus, up to his last moment, before his second death, in the midst of excruciating pain, didn't regress and nullify his first death.

If the theory of reincarnation is applied, then the second death, if the first death is achieved, symbolizes freedom from the cycle of life and death and a manifestation as an angelic being. However, if the first death isn't experienced, the second death will reintroduce the "I" into the cycle—the outcome determined by what a person sows—the good and the bad are calculated.

In the following passage, I believe Jesus is suggesting what I am of the second death, and he continues to reprimand the popular notion of the resurrection. Marriage is an act of the body's influences. The body requires marriage. The spirit does not.

> *"The same day came to him the Sadducees, which say that there is no resurrection, and asked him, Saying, Master, Moses said, If a man die, having no children, his brother shall marry his wife, and raise up seed unto his brother. Now there were with us seven brethren: and the first, when he had married a wife, deceased, and, having no issue, left his wife unto his brother: Likewise the second also, and the third, unto the seventh. And last of all the woman died also. Therefore in the resurrection whose wife shall she be of the seven? for they all had her.*
>
> *Jesus answered and said unto them, Ye do err, not knowing the scriptures, nor the power of God. For in the resurrection they neither marry, nor are given in marriage, but are as the angels of God in heaven."* — (Matthew 22:23-24)

When reading specific passages, and many there are, it feels as if the writers are actually expressing the notion of reincarnation. The above is one example and others are with the use of the word, resurrection. At times, the term refers to the rebirth of the spirit and the death of the body's influences, and at other times, the word appears to represent the idea of reincarnation.

> *"Marvel not at this: for the hour is coming, in the which all that are in the graves shall hear his voice, and shall come forth; they that have done good, unto the resurrection of life; and they that have done evil, unto the resurrection of damnation."* — (John 5:28-29)

> *"But this I confess unto thee, that after the way which they call heresy, so worship I the God of my fathers, believing all things which are written in the law and in the prophets: And have hope toward God, which they themselves also allow, that there shall be a resurrection of the dead, both of the just and unjust."* — (Acts 24:14-15)

To be honest, I'm really not that concerned, at the moment, if after the body actually dies, it's reincarnation or the popular Christian illustration, simply because each is asking the same of a person.

The commonalities prescribe one mean and all ends are reached by travelling the same road and stepping on the same stone. Whatever the fixed is, each who travels this road and steps on this stone is subject to the absolute, regardless if they were aware or unaware of the truth.

So, let it be reincarnation or Hell and Heaven. It doesn't matter. All notions hold hands, travel the same road, and step on the same stone.

Unfortunately, some Christian denominations have a hate-on for everything Eastern religion. This has prevented the correct interpretation of several *Biblical* notions. I guess these denominations fear the building of a bridge between the Christians and the East, and to divert the God seeker, fantastical alternatives are presented. Another idea, in addition to reincarnation, victimized by the artificial divide is karma.

Karma is an integral cog in the machine that is reincarnation and *the Bible* often speaks of karma.

> *"Be not deceived; God is not mocked: for whatsoever a man soweth, that shall he also reap."* — (Galatians 6:7)

Karma is linked to the principles of reincarnation. One is not without the other. When a person's ascendance occurs, a person's energy, shaped by the actions in life, determines what environment an individual will gravitate towards.

The shape or make-up of a person's energy determines to where and what their energy will again manifest. Manifestation and energy attract each other. Certain types or shapes of energy naturally attract to specific manifestations. It's all cause and effect. Even demi-gods are subject.

To navel gaze a little more, it might be that another purpose of sleep, beyond giving the body rest, is to send communications of the day's memories to the court of karma. Perhaps, the Judge of Dharma (karma) evaluates these memories to determine tomorrow's karma and a person's karma after the body perishes, in turn, introducing positive or negative energy.

It might also be that the laws that govern karma are within a person, and the human body doesn't send out communications but deliberates them within— without a person's awareness.

How else can the court of karma know everything about everyone? How else can the court of karma justify administering judgment?

According to the suggestion, karma not only plays a role in the type of daily experiences an individual encounters, karma also prescribes what type of existence a person is born to. Genetics, inherited wealth, life experiences, innate spirituality, etc., are the result of a person's past life karma.

"And even the very hairs of your head are all numbered." — (Matthew 10:30)

A person's constitution is predetermined and not random, and a person is born to a specific karma. Although there might be a day-to-day deliberation, and day-to-day causes and effects, all is predetermined beforehand. A person's karma is determined by their previous existence and the karma of their future self is determined by their current state of existence. It's an equation. There is no escaping it. It's written in the cosmos and the planets know it. Regardless of how much you think you're the author of experiences, it's actually a cognitive illusion.

This said, God scripts each living things karma, it's foreordained, and The Formless is the only able to rewrite what is written. The script can be updated, but before this can happen, the first step is to connect with God and request a revision.

Accordingly, a person is not trapped to their karma. You are not who you were and you will not be who you are. Beg The Father for perfect karma—the type that provides the best second death.

To one degree or another, most of the world's religions teach about reincarnation and karma—including the Jewish faith. The *Zohar* clearly details the concepts. However, in a few religious houses, the teachings aren't explicit, even though the ideas can be identified within their doctrine.

> *"So whatever you wish that others would do to you, do also to them, for this is the Law and the Prophets."* — (Matthew 7:12)

Books by Mike Bhangu

The Body Matrix

The Vedic demi-god, Indra, once incarnated as a pig. He did this to teach the pigs how to live a less filthy life. Indra felt, that as a pig, he might better influence the pigs than in demi-god form.

After some time, the other demi-gods took notice and descended to where Indra incarnated. They asked Indra what he was doing and to resume his place as a demi-god. Indra responded with delight for a pig's life and proceeded to tell them to leave him alone. He was happy living in waste.

The demi-gods, perplexed, eventually forced Indra out of the pig by killing the pig. Indra, in his demi-god form, laughed and laughed. He was amused by his thoughts as a pig. He loved the filth he lived in, as he thought it was the heights of living, and he could not imagine a better existence, or his being as a demi-god.

This is the mindset of a person trapped to Mammon and the body. From within the box, they do not see the rubbish they existence in and believe it as bliss. Nor do they recognize their true self, the invisible within.

The "I"

The true "I" is not the body. The body is only a temporary vehicle. The true "I" is the driver. Yet, without recognizing this, a person lives in cruise control, and the destination is determined by the body's programming and desires.

The first step before an individual can battle to release the spirit is to recognize that the body is not the true "I". The true "I" existed before this body and the true "I" will continue to be after the fall of the flesh.

Jesus' Sacrifice

Christianity propagates that Jesus sacrificed himself on the cross for the world's sins, so the world might continue to exist. A quick question—If Jesus died for the world's sins, why has humanity continued to sin? The idea doesn't truly make sense. This doesn't mean it isn't true, but I think there is more to the idea.

I believe that Jesus was persecuted, but I don't believe he sacrificed himself for the world's sins. If anything, he sacrificed himself for the Divine Truth he was attempting to communicate to those who strayed. Besides, The Almighty is powerful enough to erase the world's sins without having to engage in a blood sacrifice and all the drama surrounding it.

Not only do I not fully accept the idea of Jesus and the world's sins, I also do not believe in the notion of a blood sacrifice. Christianity proclaims that Jesus was the last blood sacrifice and no other blood sacrifices are now required. By Christianity claiming that Jesus was the last blood sacrifice, and as such, no other blood sacrifices were required to appease The Celestial, suggests that the foundation of Christianity is a human blood sacrifice.

This notion of sacrificing things to appease The Father was a method utilized in the previous age, but with the introduction of this epoch, meditation toward The Source is far more fruitful. The idea of Jesus' sacrifice is most likely symbolizing an understanding of the previous aeon.

It's more than plausible that the idea of Jesus as the last blood sacrifice also came about to persuade the Pagans that blood sacrifices were no longer necessary to appease The Celestial, and to make Christianity more attractive to the Pagans. Constantine desired to make the Roman Empire a Christian dominion, but a large portion of the kingdom was Pagan. The Roman Emperor understood that to persuade the Pagans to adopt Christianity, the Christian doctrine must be a little Pagan.

Constantine was a slick politician. He did many things to trick not only the Pagans, but also the Christians. Even his supposed vision of a cross in the sky, before a decisive battle, should be questioned. Did he invent the phenomena so to persuade the Christians that he was sanctioned by God to lead them? Constantine was a politician and it's foolish to trust his words and intentions without verification.

....

Why is the blood of Jesus considered sacred? Blood is known to carry the essence and vibrational characteristics of a being. The blood of Jesus resonates The Name and The Word. The Name and The Word are the most powerful forces in the Universe, excluding The Great-Giver. For this reason, the blood of the Christ is considered sacred.

How to Die: Salvation

Jesus is salvation by way of example. He demonstrated the twofold death.

Without dying twice, the highest existence will not be experienced. Salvation isn't easy to garnish.

You see, while alive, a person must escape Mammon's matrix and conquer the body—the metaphorical first death. Only then, when a person's body actually ceases to produce a heartbeat, the real death, will the true self ascend toward the highest existence, as an angelic being.

The true you isn't the vessel, the true you is within. The twofold death is the truest death and truly releases the true self.

Jesus is salvation. Through his example, deliverance is the end manifestation.

We allow Death to choose us, at Death's pleasure. Like a servant and not a master. The person who rises above the body develops a companionship with Death—the two walk hand-in-hand. Here, the person decides when Death with pull the "I" from the physical realm. Such an individual is a king amid slaves. Such a person is superhuman and deserving of our admiration.

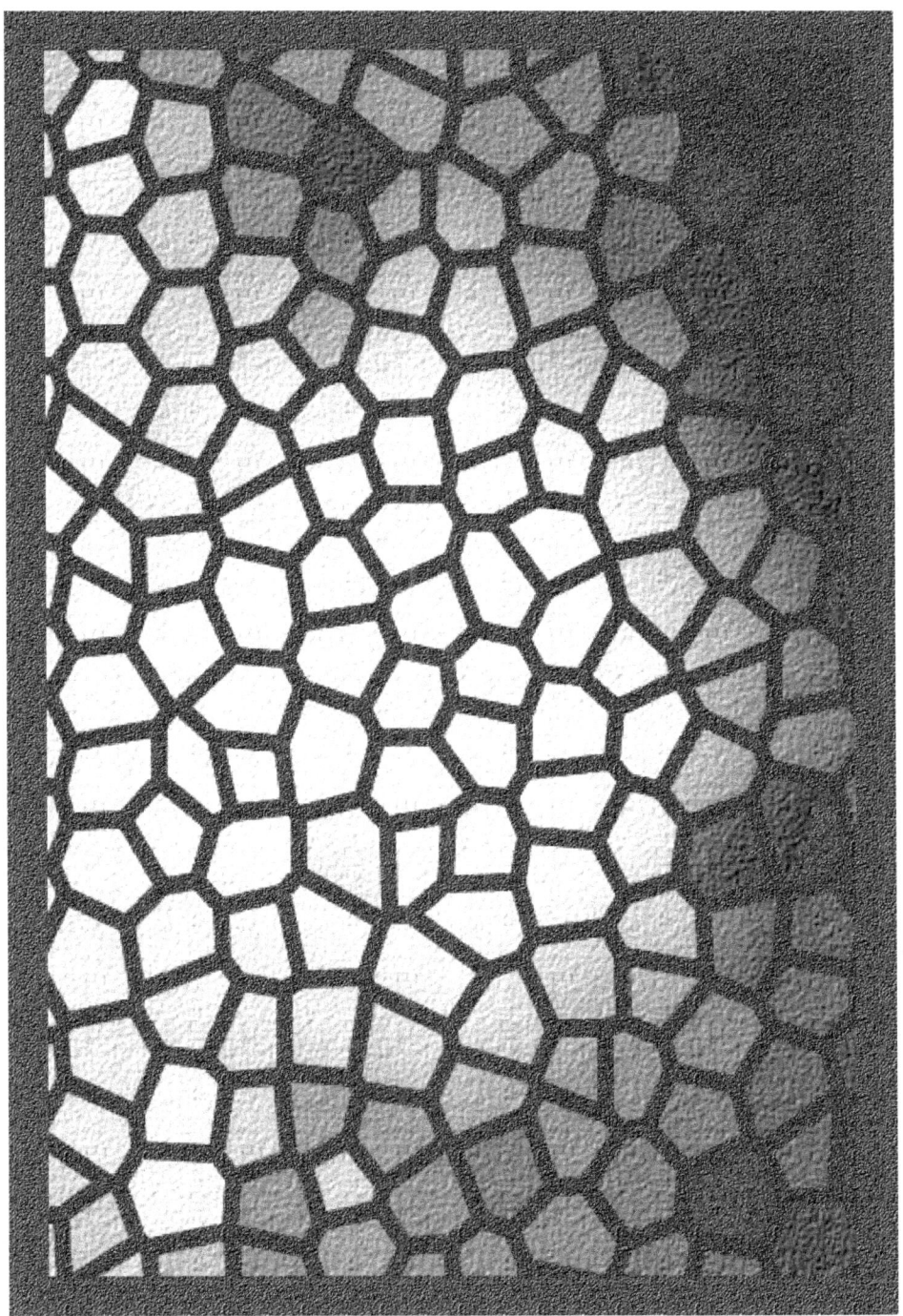

Is Jesus God?

Understand this. In whom God's Word speaks, God is one, and there is little difference between that person and The Great Architect.

When an individual reaches a state in which The Word is fully active, their identical-self consumes the self and the person essentially merges with The Lord. Such a person walks in the Will of God, in full awareness, and all that he or she says and does is the authority of The Great-Giver. Under this context, the following passages should be read.

> *(Jesus said) "I and my Father are one."* — (John 10:30)

> *(Jesus said) "Don't you believe that I am in the Father, and that the Father is in me? The words I say to you I do not speak on my own authority. Rather, it is the Father, living in me, who is doing his work."* — (John 14:10)

> *(Jesus said) "I am the Alpha and the Omega, the Beginning and the End, the First and the Last."* — (Rev 22:13)

The subsequent passage also requires proper context. The phrase was said by Jesus after he merged with The Father. It is God speaking. This doesn't mean Jesus is the only way and any person through whom God works can legitimately speak the following words.

> *"I am the way, and the truth, and the life. No one comes to the Father except through me."* — (John 14:6)

Those lucky men and women who rise above the darkness swim in The Lord's Fragrance. Moreover, they're a witness to God's great play, as opposed to a player unable to comprehend the game, or better put, the bigger picture. Until the creation merges with The Creator, God's creations are simply fulfilling their predestined motions. Trapped they are in the script, pending an intervention by The Holy Spirit.

Jesus blended with The Lord through The Word, thus Jesus was God. Yet, this doesn't mean God incarnated or that God took birth. There is a distinction between God and Jesus. Even Jesus, many times, acknowledged the difference.

(Jesus said) "And he that seeth me seeth him that sent me." — (John 12:45)

(Jesus said) "Why do you call Me good? No one is good but One, that is, God." — (Mark 10:18)

"And at the ninth hour Jesus cried out with a loud voice, saying, 'Eloi, Eloi, lama sabachthani?' which is translated, 'My God, My God, why have You forsaken Me?'" — (Mark 15:34)

(Jesus said) "Do you not believe that I am in the Father, and the Father in me? I am not myself the source of the words I speak to you: it is the Father who dwells in me doing his own work. Believe me when I say that I am in the Father and the Father in me; or else accept the evidence of the deeds themselves." — (John 14:10-11)

"Verily, verily, I say unto you, He that believes on me, the works that I do shall he do also; and greater works than these shall he do; because I go unto my Father." — (John 14: 12)

Jesus wasn't born God. Jesus became one with The Father. In my humble opinion, the second is far more difficult. It's easier to be born Pure than to become Pure. The journey is one of human suffering and Jesus is the perfect example. His life is truly inspirational. Imagine a person who understands this and strives to be as him. Imagine even one-tenth of the Christian world doing the same. The makers of worldly problems might be pushed into the ocean and held at bay. Imagine a world that mimics Heaven. This is the power of those who follow the example of Jesus and become. Jesus born as

God is an example no person can follow. To prevent a change in the division of power, is this why Jesus born God is the popular version of Jesus?

God's Word sleeps within every person, and when awake, the person is elevated above the influences of Mammon and transforms into a superhuman. In Jesus The Word was fully awake, but he wasn't the only who The Holy Ghost lifted from the pit of darkness. Others too have blended. Others too held the same status as Jesus, individuals such as Buddha and Guru Nanak. The above passages can be attributed to any of these blessed beings.

Other men and women besides Jesus too merged with The Great Architect. They too are gateways to The Father. However, several Christian denominations do not see it this way and they further propagate that anyone who doesn't give God the name, Jesus, will burn in hell. I must ask—What about the billions who existed before the birth of Jesus? They never had an opportunity to know the name, and did they all, by default, fall to hell?

I guess if God was cruel, this might be true.

Interestingly, the name, Jesus, is relatively new and for many centuries he was known to the Christians as Yesu, Yoshua, and Isa. Jesus is an alias invented after the creation of the letter "J". The letter "J" was invented in the 1500s (*Wikipedia*). What's more, and according to Michael Tsarion, *the Dead Sea Scrolls* don't even mention the name, Jesus.

The same people who believe Jesus is the only path to salvation suggest, regardless of a person's character, that by simply accepting the name, Jesus, a person's sins will be forgiven, and after death, an individual will automatically enter Heaven. However, this isn't what *the New Testament* advocates. If only the entrance to Heaven was that easy to pass through. Besides, Jesus wasn't his name.

> *"For it is easier for a camel to go through a needle's eye, than for a rich man to enter into the kingdom of God."* — (Luke 18:25)

The above passage suggests that a person caught in the net of Maya is too big to fit through the gateway to Heaven—no matter if he accepted the name, Jesus. Moreover, without The Word and The Name, the highest Heaven cannot be experienced. Without The Word and The Name, no one sits in the presence of The Father.

The True Name of God is also a sacred vibration/frequency/sound, and it too is only given by God's Spirit. Those who know it do not dare share it with another. For the person who does, death is the outcome. The Universe doesn't tolerate a chatterbox. The secret is to remain a secret. Only God determines who will receive The Name. In fear of this Universal Law, instead of writing The Name, in its place, the Jewish adepts used the four Hebrew characters known as the *Tetragrammaton*.

The mystery of God's Name, like God's Word, only came to light after studying the Sikh Holy Book. As with The Word, *Sri Guru Granth Sahib Ji* is upfront about the nature of The Name.

> *"I am a sacrifice to my True Guru (God's Spirit), who has revealed the Lord's hidden Name to me.||2||"* — (Sri Guru Granth Sahib Ji, ang 697 of 1430)

> *"Without serving the True Guru (God's Spirit), the Naam is not obtained. The Naam is the True profit in this world. || 6 || True is His Will, beauteous and pleasing through the Word of the Shabad (God's Word). The Panch Shabad, the five primal sounds, vibrate and resonate."* — (Sri Guru Granth Sahib Ji, ang 1057 of 1430)

> *"Those who are attached to the Naam, the Name of the Lord, are saved; without the Name, they must go to the City of Death.*

O Nanak, without the Name, they find no peace..." — (Sri Guru Granth Sahib Ji, ang 1415 of 1430)

After understanding how it's possible, I cannot deny the Godhood of Jesus. Nor can I deny the Godhood of others who also amalgamated. The religions claiming only one or the other as the only way to The Father do so to divide the people, and of course, to expand their monopoly over "salvation".

....

In this epoch, those as Isa are few and far between. Yet, in the Golden Age, they are many. (The Golden Age is defined in an upcoming article).

Saving the Christian?

Many Christian Churches teach the Christian that it's their duty to "save" others, by introducing them to the Church's interpretation of Jesus and *the Gospels*. The Churches further imply, by doing so, he or she is appeasing Heaven's mandate.

The story of Jesus and the messages in *the Gospels* do teach of salvation and can "save" a person. This, I cannot deny. Yet, if incorrectly decoded, or mistranslations or earthly insertions are understood as truth, false assertions will be the outcome. The God seeker will miss the mark without knowing it.

If the knowledge I share is correct, the popular interpretations imprison Christian understanding and conceal the magnitude of Jesus. Jesus is much more amazing than the fashionable versions of him. By indoctrinating others to a false interpretation, the Christian isn't emancipating their fellow human. On the contrary, they only thicken the shackles.

So, I must ask—Is it the non-Christian world that requires saving, or is it the Christians, from the many erroneous readings of Jesus' life and *the Gospels*?

"Woe to you, scribes and Pharisees, hypocrites! For you travel land and sea to win one proselyte, and when he is won, you make him twice as much a son of hell as yourselves." — (Matthew 23:15)

If no Jesus: Heaven vs. Heaven

If no Abraham,
if no Moses,
if no Jesus,
if no Mohammad,
if no Nanak,
would there be The One?

If no *Gospels*,
if no *Qur'an*,
if no *Gathas*,
if no *Guru Granth*,
would there be God?

Why do we allow for the divisions when in the beginning and the end, there is only ONE? We reinforce the divisions because each believes that they're the only with the truth. Each believes that their prophet, or their God-Like, or their book is the absolute.

But all prophets, God-Like, and Holy Books have much in common. It's a matter of understanding the language, symbols, and context. Appreciate that each of the holy from the many religions performed miracles, each Holy Book reveals The Eternal, and countless people have utilized the teaches of each religion as a gateway to The Absolute.

So, why are the religions on opposite ends?

After moving aside generations of political spin and digging through centuries of religious riddles, most religious institutions claim superiority for several reasons:

    1) To empower the elite and their agenda.
    2) To reinforce the religious institution's reputation as the only holder of divine truth.

3) To instil a sense of superiority within the followers and to pit them against another group.
4) And to sanction the believer to war, to conquer, and to loot.

It's much easier to convince good people to war against other people when they believe the other represents a false prophet, book, or god. It's much easier to convince a people to war if they feel they're freeing another people from their false prophet, book, or god. And it's much easier to convince a people to war if they feel that The Formless guides only them.

Many popular religions proclaim that they are absolute, and it's my belief that politics played centuries ago, today, prevent those religions from acknowledging the others. But regardless of what those religious institutions may believe, no matter the centuries that divide the baker and the cake, the root to all true religions is the same. Besides, a rose is still a rose no matter the name.

....

Religions were hijacked long ago by those who rule. I haven't encountered a single religion that isn't ill. Religions are sick and there is a mix of political intentions and true doctrine. The book, *War and Religion*, further examines the infiltration.

> "Jesus said, 'The Pharisees and the scribes have taken the keys of Knowledge and hidden them. They themselves have not entered, nor have they allowed to enter those who wish to. You, however, be as wise as serpents and as innocent as doves.'" — (Gospel of Thomas)

If Jesus was a Mortal Man

Jesus was God in the sense that he merged with The Great-Giver. But Jesus is spoken of, by half the Christian world, as if he was born as The Great Architect. Jesus was born a mortal man, and by conquering Mammon, Jesus evolved into the Christ. So, why is Jesus' evolution, and the extraordinary trials and tribulations he overcame to rise above the masses, denied?

If depicted as a mortal man, who sacrificed himself in the struggle for the greater good and for a better world, the common person might get the idea that he or she can do it too. A mortal Jesus might inspire others to bring about positive social change and to resist an oppressive status quo.

Moreover, Jesus demonstrated that a mortal is able to merge with The Word and access the superhuman abilities that accompany the sacred vibration. Jesus illustrated that a common person can become strong enough, by conquering the body and allowing the spirit to solely influence Thought Energy, to stand against the likes of the Roman Empire.

Sheep might mutate into divine lions, if they understand the potential of the human creature. This prospective is in every human being and it's advantageous for the rulers to hide this power from those they wish to control.

The Roman ruling class and the early Catholic Church, under which the Christian doctrine was solidified over a millennia ago, didn't want to inspire the common person to ask the questions—If Jesus can do it, why can't I? If a mortal man can do it, why can't I? The Emperor and the religious elite didn't benefit by promoting Jesus as a revolutionary martyr, who harnessed the power of the Universe and challenged the rulers. That idea might inspire a socially conscious revolution, ignited by an army powered by The Word. No force on Earth can withstand such a union. Empires fall before them. I know of one such army, the Khalsa, and they crushed those considered uncrushable.

The Khalsa was an army of saint-soldiers, and many, many of this covenant's members overpowered Mammon and utilized the power of the spiritual world. Instituted in 1699 by Guru Gobind Singh, a man in whom The Word resonated and a man who also merged with The Great Architect, the Khalsa came about to battle tyranny. The non-Muslims of India were facing extermination at the hands of the Mughal intruders. The Khalsa was formed to prevent this from happening. After the destruction of the Mughals, the Afghans decided to invade and they too were smashed by the Khalsa.

Against all worldly forces, the Khalsa rose like a Phoenix to illuminate the darkness, but only because the Khalsa's members followed the example of Guru Gobind Singh.

By all accounts, the people who first joined the Khalsa were weak men and women. They were from the poor and uneducated classes. Whereas, the Mughal Empire was the richest empire the world is yet to see, and the Afghans were rarely defeated. But thousands of instances witnessed a few Khalistanis battling incredible odds, such as the forty men, along with Guru Gobind, who fought a one-million man army sent to annihilate them—Battle of Mukstar—December 29, 1705. The Great Gobind walked away from the battlefield without a scratch. That is the power of The Word. Gobind was scar-less and sheep were transformed into divine lions. Mystically, Guru Gobind was able to enhance a person's physical presence and strength. The story of Bachittar Singh and Deep Singh will demonstrate.

Guru Gobind, a Son of God (defined in an upcoming article), fought many battles, lost none, and in one, while in the fort of Anandpur Sahib, he was surrounded by the combined army of the Hill-Chiefs and the Mughals. After an unsuccessful two months, the Hill-Chiefs and Mughals decided to break through the main gate of the fort and attack. They intoxicated a war elephant and directed the elephant towards the gate.

On hearing of the oncoming attack, the Guru asked one of his soldiers, Bachittar Singh, to ride out and meet the elephant. Without any hesitation, Bachittar, with a single lancer, left the safety of the fort and rushed out to meet the charging beast. From horseback, he struck the gigantic elephant with such a powerful blow that it penetrated the steel armour covering the elephant's face. The elephant was stopped in its tracks, and then surprisingly, it turned around and attacked the aggressors. At which point, the main gate of the fort opened from within and the Khalsa rushed out and crushed the enemy.

In the year 1757, Ahmad Shah Abdali invaded India for the fourth time, and on his return home, he was constantly harassed by the Sikhs. In retaliation, Ahmad Shah Abdali ordered the plundering and capture of Amritsar. On hearing of this tragedy, Deep Singh and a band of Sikhs vowed to retake the city.

On their march towards the city, they battled many Afghan soldiers, and during one skirmish, Deep Singh received a blow to the neck that virtually severed his head from his body. But miraculously, and on hearing the cries of the Sikhs who followed him into battle, Deep Singh managed to hold his head in place with his left hand, while he fought his way through the Afghan soldiers with a sword in the other. He eventually fell, but not before defeating the Afghans and reaching Amritsar.

There are thousands of stories, and I'm not exaggerating, of the Khalsa overcoming incredible odds to win the day. Guru Gobind Singh truly transformed mice into titans. Now, I'm not suggesting that every member of the Khalsa was blessed with an active Word. Yet, all it takes is one with a quasi-wake Word to empower every believer around him or her.

Jesus was a Divine spirit but I think this idea of Jesus as something more than a human being is a plausible political injection. Jesus was eventually depicted as born God to prevent the memory of Jesus from inspiring the common person to do as Jesus.

The idea of "turning the other cheek" was also plausibly changed when *the New Testament* was consolidated. There must be more to the idea.

There were times when Jesus didn't turn the other cheek. For instance, Jesus opposed the immoral idea of collecting taxes in a place of worship. Instead of turning the other cheek, Jesus, like a champion, rushed the Jewish Temple and flipped a few tables. By his actions, Jesus communicated that there are times when it isn't righteous to turn the other cheek.

By indoctrinating the notion of "turning the other cheek" without the idea further explained, the Emperor and the Catholic Church were able to potentially subdue any effective resistance before an effective resistance came into existence. Christian lions turned into political sheep by the ruling classes.

Jesus is delineated as more than mortal and this is to deny the common people of their power, and their ability to change the world so the world can be a better place. There is a division within society, between the rulers and the ruled, and the ruled must be kept weak if the rulers wish to continue their rule.

Eggs, Bunnies, and Jesus

Pagan ideas pollute the House of Jesus, but how many know it?

What originally was is hidden. What we have is an alteration. This due to Emperor Constantine's interference. The Roman Emperor tampered with the ways of Jesus and blended Pagan ideas, from the Mithra tradition, with Christian concepts.

Scholars suggest that Constantine, when he converted the Roman Empire from a Pagan Empire to a Christian Kingdom, behaved more as a politician than a Christian. The Pagans were powerful enough to burn the Roman Empire to the ground, and to avert a civil war, Constantine allowed Pagan ideas to continue, such as idolizing the bones of dead saints.

Moreover, the blending of ideas was a way to distort Christian truths and their nature to empower a common person. The symbol of the cross with a circle is another example of the marriage (in some schools, it represents the Pagan Sun god), the idea of Trinity existed before Jesus but with different characters, many of the first Catholic priests were Pagans, and the Vatican is built on ancient Pagan spiritual land.

In my opinion, the celebration of Easter is one of the most evident examples of the mix, but tragically, most Christians don't see it, even though the popular elements of Easter are not in *the New Testament*. Lent, eggs, egg hunts, bunnies, etc. aren't anywhere in the Holy Book. Furthermore, the original apostles and early *New Testament* Church, before it was hijacked, didn't even acknowledge Easter.

The elements of Easter seem to stem from the worship of the Babylonian goddess Ishtar. Ishtar is pronounced as you would the word, Easter. Ishtar also resurrected—as with several others from around the world. As with the others, her resurrection included the defeat of the body and the rebirth of the spirit.

The ancient Babylonians depicted Ishtar as a powerful warrior goddess, who conquered the strongest. However, Ishtar is popularly known as the goddess of fertility, and she's commonly worshipped in the spring since that season symbolizes the renewal of life. With time, an association evolved between eggs and fertility, and eggs were eventually incorporated into the worship of Ishtar.

Now, the Bunny doesn't come from the same place the egg does. Bunnies are a remnant of the festival of Eostre, a great Northern goddess. Or, Eostre and Ishtar are the same deity but initially worshipped differently by different nations. The Sumerians supposedly called Ishtar, Inanna.

To appease the large Pagan population not willing to forget their Pagan roots and to conceal truths, the Roman Empire compromised and allowed Pagan elements to mix with Christian doctrine. This said, in the case of Inanna, if her spirit was the dominant influence over her thoughts and actions, this would suggest that The Word was active within her. She too was a possible Christ. This can only mean that even in the Pagan ways, there is truth. As with the contemporary Christian world, the Pagan world eventually evolved to house falsehoods, but Pagan roots are most likely pure. It's the falsehoods that require expiration. There's nothing wrong with acknowledging the truthful Pagan elements. The truth is the truth, no matter the house it rests in.

The other popular religions of the world also support some form of false Paganism. The different doctrines of Paganism were the standard before the emergence of monolithic religions and the initial converts to the popular religions were Pagan. It's highly likely that many did not completely abandon their original beliefs when they converted.

Plausibility begins to lose its validity when discussing if Pagan ideas infiltrated the House of Jesus. Without a good teacher or many years of self-study, a person is at a disadvantage and he or she will not fully distinguish between Paganism and the teachings of Jesus.

The Original Sabbath

Did you know, Sunday is not the day Sabbath was first practiced.

Sabbath on Sunday was introduced during Rome's take-over of the Christian nation. The original Sabbath is Saturday. It was changed to Sunday to align with the day the Sun god was worshipped by the Pagans.

Supposedly, Sabbath, on a Saturday, is so to adore the planet Saturn. The Ancient world believed that each of the visible planets is a living being with duties, and each is able to emit influence over a person's existence. Saturn's duty is to teach a person lessons, and sometimes, lessons are taught the hard way. Saturn, to teach, might obstruct a person in their endeavours and activities. If this is the case, it doesn't matter how much effort a person exerts toward their endeavour or activity, Saturn's influence will not allow him or her to reach a completion.

To gain Saturn's favour, and to request Saturn assist a person in their activities, the ancient world dedicated Saturday, Sabbath, to Saturn worship.

....

The seven visible planets, including the Moon and the Sun, are the archangels. Also referred to as Elohim. Correctly translated into English, the word, Elohim, means gods and not God. These seven are the seven spirits spoken of in *Revelation*, also denoted as the seven stars. *Revelation* further speaks of seven churches and these are a person's seven dominant energy centers, also coined the seven seals.

The Sun God

Those who deny the existence of Jesus and suggest that Jesus actually references the Sun god, use valid arguments to support their position.

December 25th isn't the day Jesus was born but the day the Sun god is reborn. The term, the Saviour of the World, and, the Saviour of mankind, were employed by the pre-Jesus world to denote the Sun god. And so on.

Moreover, the twelve disciples do represent the Zodiac, and it might be that the Jewish people are correct and there were only five principle disciples with Jesus. Nor in *the Dead Sea Scrolls* are the twelve disciples mentioned. The year zero doesn't denote the year Jesus was born but the year the current Cosmic Month, Pisces, rose as the dominant constellation. The emblem of the fish symbolizes this.

The above are all true. Some characteristics of Jesus and his life are used to symbolize astrological bodies and movements. This is due to the merger between Christian and Pagan thought. It was a try at appeasing two distinct religious populations with one stone. As such, a Pagan will read his or her belief system, and the Christian, in the same passages, will see Jesus.

It's impressive what those who compiled *the New Testament* were able to do, but this doesn't mean that Jesus didn't exist. Do not be fooled by the mix. Isa is Christ.

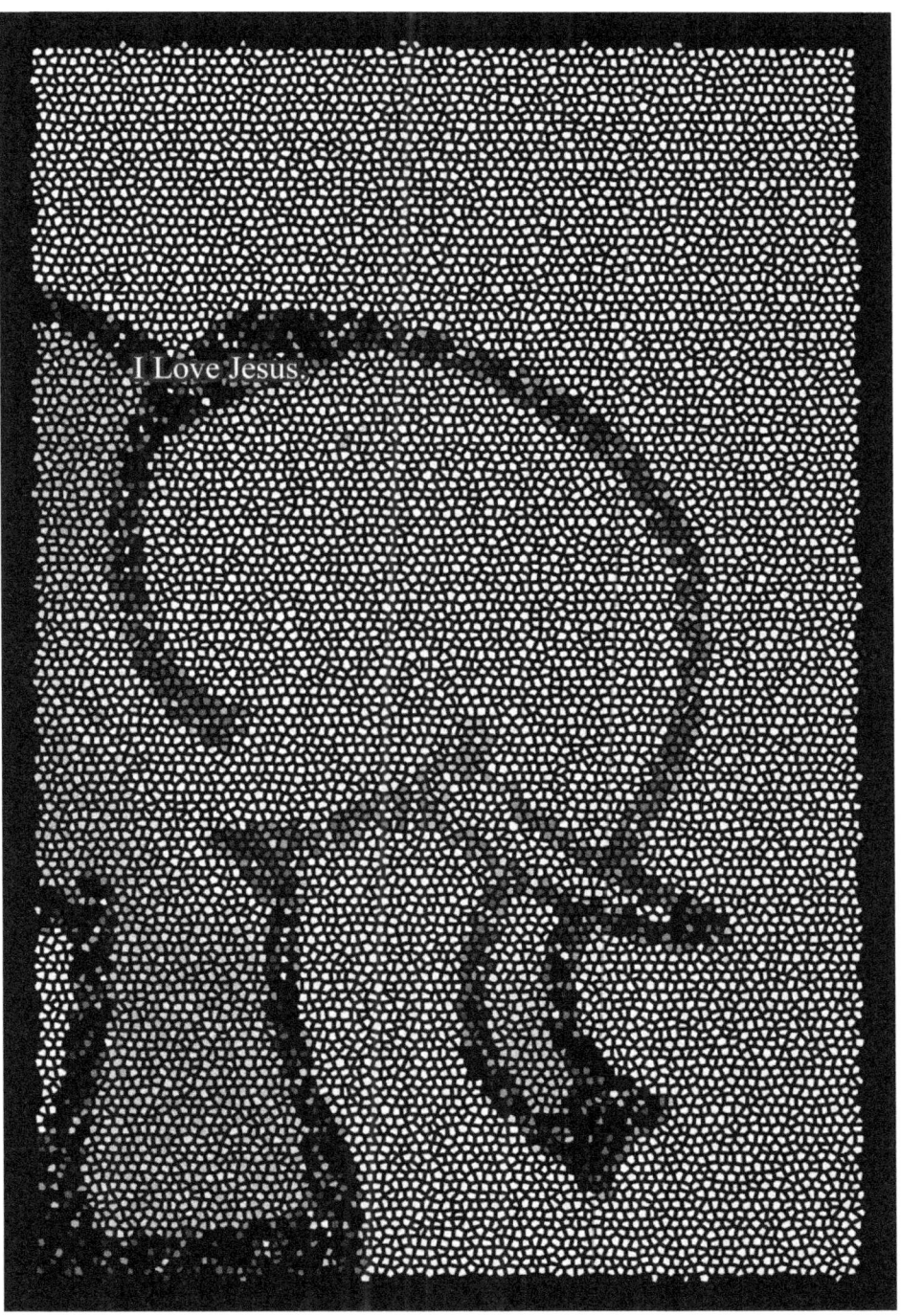

God is Within

The Eternal Commander and Chief created all, and in doing so, The Eternal infused The Essence that is God within everything that exists. Without this Essence, there would be nothing to support the Universe and all its principles and inhabitants, including the human condition's breath of life. For this reason, every single human being is equal to another.

This idea of God within the individual troubles one of the most popular religions, and I think it's because they don't fully understand the notion. It seems as if the belief of God within the human condition implies to Christendom that the person is God. However, this isn't the case. God is within all creation and separate from (onto Thyself).

Not surprisingly, the above notion wasn't foreign to the Christian's before Constantine created *the New Testament,* especially amid the Gnostics. But Constantine didn't like the idea. Such ideas might discourage the Christian from invading other people's places, taking their possessions, murdering them, and stealing their land to expand the Roman Empire. To hurt another is to hurt the God within them, and why would anyone who appreciates the idea endeavour to hurt another knowing The Primal Void also feels it?

> *"Jesus said, 'If they say to you -where did you come from? Say to them—we came from the light, the place where the light came into being on its own accord and established [itself] and became manifest through their image. If they say to you—is it you? Say—we are its children, we are the elect of the Living Father. If they ask you—what is the sign of your father in you? Say to them—it is movement and repose.'"* — (Gospel of Thomas)

Countless saints have spoken of God in such a manner. Great philosophers such as Aristotle and Pythagoras too expressed the idea. The All-Mind is within all minds.

They further suggested that to discover The Light within (God's Essence) is one of the highest life purposes.

The purpose is to allow The Light (God) within to govern the mind and body so to eventually merge with The Supreme Light. When The Light within is discovered, nurtured, and finally merged with The Supreme Light, an individual is considered one with The Primal Void and The Primal Void is considered one with the individual. If an individual does reach this state of being, there is little difference between the two. Moreover, he or she is no longer subject to the principles of the Universe that govern life and death. The potential for immortality is the individual's but not immortality of the physical. Death can be overcome.

So, search for The Light within, God is closer to you than some popular religions have propagated. As Jesus expressed, the true church is within the body fortress.

Jesus didn't require a church to build a relationship with The Formless. The people also do not require a church to link with God. But this notion threatens the power of those who operate religious institutions and it's in their interest to change who Jesus was so Jesus doesn't threaten their status.

> *"Neither shall they say, Lo here! or, lo there! for, behold, the kingdom of God is within you."* — (Luke 17:21)

God is within and there's a concentration of the God Essence within the heart and the heart chakra. The Egyptians believed so strongly in this idea that when they mummified a dead body, they would throw away the brain and pay overwhelming attention to the heart. The heart was more valuable than the brain.

The Egyptians were not and are not the only people who give the heart and the heart chakra importance. Most other spiritual paths that utilize the chakras of the human condition also accommodate the same understanding.

"Wherever I look, I see that One Lord alone. Deep within each and every heart, He Himself is contained. ||1||Pause||" — (Sri Guru Granth Sahib Ji, ang 387 of 1430)

If you can, listen to the heart and think from the heart—allow the information within the heart chakra to influence the time and space of thought.

The person is a body fortress and within is The Great Architect. Not only that, the human body is constituted by divine instruments such as the Ida, Pingali, and Sushmana. These three instruments are pathways within the body and they're able to reveal the spiritual realm. With meditative intention, a person's breath is used to travel through these channels, but only after an individual has developed a heightened awareness. Beforehand, a person should not experiment. It's dangerous.

The Eternal Commander and Chief created all, and in doing so, The Eternal infused the Essence that is God within everything that exists. Without this Essence, there would be nothing to support the Universe and all its principles and inhabitants.

....

The popular religions believe that all creation sprung from God's Word, God's Breath, or God separated Thy Self. They all claim that creation came from a singular point. If this is true, then nothing within the Universe is without elements from this singular point of creation. Thus, God must also be within. But please don't be mistaken, there is only ONE.

The Best Time to Pray

In the 24-hour cycle, certain hours are better for prayer and meditation.

Pray or meditate during the early of the night. The Sikh people call this moment, Amrit Vela. The holy people suggest that then is the ideal time because the person isn't exposed to the rays of the Sun. The power of the Sun interferes with a meditative state—it energizes the body's influences. The body must be silenced to achieve a true meditative state. Moreover, the energy the Earth absorbed from the Sun, during the day, is released at night but in a different form, and this energy enhances the practice of prayer and meditation.

> *"Now in the morning, having risen a long while before daylight, He (Jesus) went out and departed to a solitary place; and there He prayed."* — (Mark 1:35)

> *"When I remember You on my bed, I meditate on You in the night watches."* — (Psalm 63:6)

> *"My eyes are awake through the night watches, that I may meditate on Your word."* — (Psalm 119:148)

Some Christian denominations frown upon meditation, but if *the New Testament* is correct, Luke 17:21, and the Kingdom of God is within, a journey through the self is required to find it. Meditation is the only method to travel within the self.

> *"I will meditate on Your precepts, and contemplate Your ways. I will delight myself in Your statutes; I will not forget Your word."* — (Psalm 119:15-16)

> *"May my meditation be sweet to Him; I will be glad in the Lord."* — (Psalm 104:34)

Son of God

What is a Son of God?

Some Christian researchers suggest that the Sons of God, spoken of in *the Bible*, are the offspring of the Nephilim, fallen angels, who mixed with the Daughters of Men. They were literal giants who roamed the Earth. These researchers also assert that the term, Son of God, cites Jesus as an actual and only Son of The Father.

In *the Bible*, some characters are clear symbols and some are not. With respect to oddities as giants, Michael A. Cremo and Richard L. Thompson suggest that the archaeological establishment has discovered the skeletal remains of human giants. They continue to assert that the discoveries are not popular because the findings contradict Darwin's Theory of Evolution. An assumption that isn't completely truthful—discussed further in the book, *Angel vs. Demon*.

The Bible isn't the only that speaks of giants. Cultures from around the world share stories of titans who once walked the Earth. The ancient Indians, Sumerians, Greeks, Chinese, Aboriginal Americans, and so on, all tell stories of giants. Some of these stories have taken on a fictional aura and these stories were slowly embellished and given the characteristics common to a myth. Yet, this isn't how the tales were first told or read.

Nevertheless, I don't agree with those who believe the Sons of God were the same giants the ancient world tells of. Nor do *the Gospels* support this assertion. The term, Son of God, was used differently by the old world and as *the Gospels* were written.

The ancients of the world denoted an individual deserving of the title, Christ, a Son of God. Sons of God were the highest spiritual adepts. When Jesus is referred to as a Son of God, it's as an advanced spiritual master. This doesn't mean Jesus was conceived by The Source or that he was born a Son of The Great Architect.

With this understanding, Jesus was a Son of God, and because he merged, he was also The Father.

The term, Sons of God, refers to more than one spiritual master. Supposedly, the Sons of God ruled parts of the ancient world—preflood. In the epoch prior to the one we suffer in. The Divine right to rule was theirs. Guided by the Holy Spirit, they built civilizations.

It should be noted that the depiction of giants in the old literature sometimes symbolizes these spiritual adepts, for they were giants in mind and spirit. When it comes to determining if something is symbolic or not, the more a person knows of the ancient spiritual schools, the more symbols he or she will decode and more of *the Bible* will be understood.

The age that shelters the most Sons of God is the first, with each king as a Son. In each proceeding age, they become fewer in number. Not all the kings of the previous age were Sons of God.

In the Sumerian tradition, as translated by Zecharia Sitchin, these Sons of God were the Annunaki and possible extra-terrestrials. However, I'm not convinced. This isn't what the other ancient cultures are suggesting such as the Egyptians, Indians, and Mayans. The notion of spiritual adepts living on Earth and wisely ruling kingdoms, as ideal leaders, more so reverberates with my understanding of the old world than aliens ruling mankind.

The Sons of God, the adepts, in the previous age, were forced to ascend, but before they did, they decided to create children with the Daughters of Men—the non-adepts.

With the coming of the next age, the cosmic vibrations would corrupt their constitution. If they stayed, they would fall back into the body and the spirit would become secondary—they would no longer hold their status as spiritual adepts. The vibrations of the aeon they lived in permitted them to be as they were and to link with The Father. They walked in God's Will. The vibrations of this epoch, the age they decided to forego, do not favour the Christ and student-initiates. That's why few Christs—few Sons of God—have blessed this planet in the past 5000 years. The cosmic energies do not favour their survival. Thus, they ascended to occasionally descend as a person. In their kindness, before leaving, they decided to create offspring, so the spiritual essence within their blood might remain on Earth and provide hope. The era we exist in, the Age of Iron, is a time of spiritual ignorance. The Universe allows for this. In danger are those who attempt to walk the saintly path. The world works against them. The world attempts to destroy them. The world is in darkness. So suggest almost all the ancient cultures I studied.

As alluded to by the Vedic literature, although the cosmic radiation of this age isn't ideal for the Sons of God, it's a radiation other types of life thrive on. Supposedly, as the Sons of God ascended, with no spiritual adepts to protect the planet from an invasion, the material-minded creation descended to Earth. These beings are said to be without the beautiful half of the mind and very much servants and enjoyers of Mammon. Other ancient literature suggests that these life forms didn't descend but came from within the Earth. Yet, others tell that these beings came from another dimension. Perhaps, these stories are not to be taken literal. Maybe, they aren't referring to something more than human. It might be that these stories are allegorical and discussing the full fall of the spirit to the body, or the full rise of the body over the spirit.

The post-flood ancient Egyptians, Hopis, Indians, Greeks, Mayans, and Romans all valued this idea of the different epochs, with Greek philosophy hosting an additional age, the Age of Heroes. The Indians named each era a Yug (Yuga), the Hopis used the word, World, and the Mayans labelled each epoch a Sun.

The ancient people of the world believed that the solar system continuously cycles through four ages. Each era produces a different type of civilization, as determined by the distance between humanity and God. In the first age, the people are closest to God and there exists only one religion. All people have God knowledge and all people are wardens of a God-Consciousness.

However, with each proceeding age, the people regress and move further from God, God knowledge, and a God-Consciousness.

The forth epoch is said to be the darkest of all and furthest from the era of perfect existence. It's a time of dark influences and home to untruths. To one degree or another, almost all institutions facilitate falsehoods. This includes the culture and the intelligence filled and shaped by those institutions, and every person who makes contact with them. Furthermore, the Universe is predisposed to sway a person's consciousness to favour the beast within the person over the angelic. The fourth age is the era humanity is currently in.

The four ages are as follows. The Golden Age of Sat Yuga, the Silver Age of Trayta Yuga (Ram existed in this era), the Brass Age of Dwaapar Yuga (Krishna existed in this era), and the Iron Age of Kali Yuga (also called the Age of Darkness).

> *"In the Golden Age of Sat Yuga, everyone embodied contentment and meditation; religion stood upon four feet. With mind and body, they sang of the Lord, and attained supreme peace. In their hearts was the spiritual wisdom of the Lord's Glorious Virtues. Their wealth was the spiritual wisdom of the Lord's Glorious Virtues; the Lord was their success, and to live as Gurmukh was their glory. Inwardly and outwardly, they saw only the One Lord God; for them there was no other second. They centered their consciousness lovingly on the Lord, Har, Har. The Lord's Name was their companion, and in the Court of the Lord, they obtained honor. In the Golden Age of Sat Yuga, everyone embodied contentment and meditation; religion stood upon four feet. || 1 || Then came the Silver Age of Trayta Yuga; men's minds were ruled by power, and they practiced celibacy and self-discipline. The fourth foot of religion dropped off, and three remained. Their hearts and minds were inflamed with anger. Their hearts and minds were filled with the horribly poisonous essence of anger. The kings fought their wars and*

obtained only pain. Their minds were afflicted with the illness of egotism, and their self-conceit and arrogance increased. If my Lord, Har, Har, shows His Mercy, my Lord and Master eradicates the poison by the Guru's Teachings and the Lord's Name. Then came the Silver Age of Trayta Yuga; men's minds were ruled by power, and they practiced celibacy and self-discipline. || 2 || The Brass Age of Dwaapar Yuga came, and people wandered in doubt. The Lord created the Gopis and Krishna. The penitents practiced penance, they offered sacred feasts and charity, and performed many rituals and religious rites. They performed many rituals and religious rites; two legs of religion dropped away, and only two legs remained. So many heroes waged great wars; in their egos they were ruined, and they ruined others as well. The Lord, Compassionate to the poor, led them to meet the Holy Guru. Meeting the True Guru, their filth is washed away. The Brass Age of Dwaapar Yuga came, and the people wandered in doubt. The Lord created the Gopis and Krishna. || 3 || The Lord ushered in the Dark Age, the Iron Age of Kali Yuga; three legs of religion were lost, and only the fourth leg remained intact. Acting in accordance with the Word of the Guru's Shabad, the medicine of the Lord's Name is obtained. Singing the Kirtan of the Lord's Praises, divine peace is obtained. The season of singing the Lord's Praise has arrived; the Lord's Name is glorified, and the Name of the Lord, Har, Har, grows in the field of the body. In the Dark Age of Kali Yuga, if one plants any other seed than the Name, all profit and capital is lost. Servant Nanak has found the Perfect Guru, who has revealed to him the Naam within his heart and mind. The Lord ushered in the Dark Age, the Iron Age of Kali Yuga; three legs of religion were lost, and only the fourth leg remained intact. || 4 || 4 || 11 || " — (Sri Guru Granth Sahib Ji, ang 445-446 of 1430)

The term "Guru", used in the above passage, refers to God's Spirit and not a person. The name "Har, Har" is a name used to denote God. The Sikh Holy Text uses many different names to reference God.

In the ages prior, not only are people more God oriented, with the highest orientation during the Golden Age, men and women lived longer, people were in tune with their psychic abilities, nature wasn't so alien, a greater variety of intelligent life roamed the planet, and the Earth was more giving.

There are a few theories to how long each epoch will last. Some suggest 100 000s of years. In specific, certain schools believe that the Golden Age lasts for 1 728 000 years, the Silver for 1 296 000 years, the Bronze for 864 000 years, and the Dark lasts 432 000 years. Others suggest a Comic Year— about 26 000 Earth years.

To what happens next, there are two theories. One suggests that the cycle starts again with Sat Yuga. Another theory suggests that the cycle doesn't begin again with Sat Yuga but instead descends after Kali Yuga passes.

Interestingly, the theory of the four ages provides an answer to a question troubling mainstream historians. They don't know or don't believe how the early civilizations, such as the Egyptians, gained the knowledge that allowed them to spontaneously civilize. They've even gone as far as to suggest that aliens were responsible for their advancement. Yet, according to the ancient Egyptians, the knowledge required to civilize came from the previous ages, and it was knowledge that survived the transition from one era to another. The Sphinx is said to be from the previous age. Geologists have determined that the Sphinx is actually older than 10 000 years. They've determined this by examining the weathering the Sphinx has experienced. The examination determined that the Sphinx was exposed to rain and the Sahara hasn't experienced rainfall in over 10 000 years. If this is true, then the civilizations of this age are not as advanced as the civilizations of the past. We're playing catch-up. The supposition reminds me of a particular idea found in the Christian doctrine:

> "What has been is what will be, and what has been done is what will be done; there is nothing new under the sun." — (Ecclesiastes 1:4-11)

It should be mentioned that before the introduction of each of the four eras, and before an age begins a decline, there happens a large-scale catastrophic event such as a deluge that erases the majority of a civilization (people, culture, architecture, knowledge, technology, etc). Catastrophic world events take place before the introduction of an era to wipe clear what is. Each era gives birth to a new type of civilization, and for the new to fully be, in this case, the old must be near-erased. The Mayans believed that human civilizations were wiped-out five times already. The Sikh book, *Dasam Granth,* suggests approximately 21-22 times. In the Sikh accounts, at the end of each epoch, The Holy Spirit incarnates and assists humanity through the transition to the upcoming aeon. This includes re-establishing civilization. Two or three incarnations were in female form. It isn't aliens who stimulate the evolution of civilization, as suggested by the Ancient Alien Theorists, God's Spirit does. Ancient Alien Theorists do present facts but draw far-fetched associations and fail to appreciate what the ancient people recorded as their history. The human being, with the help of Heaven, is responsible for the greatness. Ancient Alien Theorists do more to misdirect than reveal the mysteries of our forgotten past.

At the end of each age, there also happens a grand battle, between what's considered good and what's considered evil. All the notable kings and their armies typically assemble. In the previous epoch, as recorded in *the Mahabharata*, the longest epic-poem—longer and greater than the *Iliad*—God's Spirit incarnated as Krishna. Krishna assisted the side considered good. *The Ramayana,* another epic tale originating from the now dead Indus Valley civilization (Punjab), describes the monstrous battle that ushered in the Bronze Age. At that time, The Holy Ghost incarnated as Ram.

> *"For I know that my redeemer liveth, and that he shall stand at the latter day upon the earth:"* — (Job 19:25)

Accordingly, the coming Redeemer has come before and never truly left. At the end of this epoch, the Redeemer, God's Spirit, will manifest and assist.

With respect to this age, cultures from around the world claim that their ancestors experienced civilization-destroying deluges. Science also suggests that the world has experienced multiple large-scale floods. Fortunately, even though civilizations were annihilated, pockets of people survived their respective deluge.

After learning of the many floods the world has experienced, I'm inclined to believe that Noah and his family were one of those pockets. But this idea of Noah and his family as the only survivors is a political injection.

For example, the Sumer story of Ziusudra, the Indian story of Manu, the Greek story of Deucalion, and the Babylonian story of Utnapishtim all describe a man, who inspired by Heaven, built a boat so to survive a forthcoming flood. Some stories also detail a sea vessel capable of holding vast numbers of life. You might be inclined to think that all the tales are referring to one event and the same people, but the characteristics of each story are different from the next. There were multiple survivors besides Noah and his family.

The idea, as with others, is presented as such, with Noah's family as the sole survivors, so to persuade people that the religion Noah's story stems from is associated with the only people in the world who were permitted to live by God. The idea is designed to manipulate the patron to believe those not of their house are inferior and false. Unfortunately, enough generations have recycled the lie that now a falsehood is taken as absolute and above rational discussion.

The Mayan deluge story, and the depiction of the pre-flood world, reveals a fascinating notion that's also found in Christendom. The sacred book of the Maya, *the Popol Vuh,* tells a story of a devastating flood in which the first beings were destroyed. The Mayans and many other ancient cultures from around the world, such as the Vedic culture, suggest that in the distant past, the demi-gods experimented and modified creatures. The first several creations were of an inferior character and eliminated—possibly by flood. It's said that almost all the giants of old were also lost to the oceans.

In each age, the alignment of the planets is different from the others and it's the change in the arrangement of the planets that stimulates catastrophic world events. In the Age of Sat Yug, in relation to the Earth, Venus and Saturn play a much more dominant role. The symbol of Islam possibly reflects this idea. Supposedly, the symbol is not of the Moon and Sun, but of Venus and Saturn. Islam is remembering a time of perfect existence.

Other mysteries are also put into perspective when the theory of the four ages is applied to them. For example, the questions surrounding the megalithic structures found all over the world become less when considering the eras. It's possible that they were designed the sizes they were, in a previous age, to survive catastrophic world events brought forth by the transition from one epoch to another. Perhaps, Heaven inspired as Heaven motivated Noah, but instead of a boat, instructions were provided to build huge stone structures.

Whereas ships such as Noah's stored life, the megalithic structures of the world might be designed to give knowledge. They just have to be looked at in the right light. For example, they give accurate astrological readings, their proportions are precise and mathematically arranged, they exhibit signs that advanced technology was used to make them, and they're built on what the Chinese call dragon lines (Earth energy lines). It's also possible they were designed to store written knowledge in the form of books and such, and that knowledge was retrieved after a catastrophic event. Perhaps, a storehouse of knowledge is yet to be recovered.

Ships and megalithic buildings are not the only type of structures supposedly inspired by Heaven to survive an upcoming natural disaster. For example, in the second chapter of *the Vendidad*, a division of the Zoroastrian holy book, *Avesta,* God warned the Persian King, Yima, the son of Vivanghat, of an upcoming natural disaster. God further instructed him to build underground cities and take shelter. Derinkuyu, the massive underground city discovered in Turkey, which can house as many as twenty-thousand people and the required livestock, is said to be one of the cities Yima built.

Elaborate underground cities, complexes, and tunnel systems are not all that strange. The ancient cultures from all over the world share one story or another detailing such things. For example, the Hopi and the Apache Indians believe that their ancestors once lived underground, and only after a great calamity, did they resurface.

In his book, *Weird America*, Jim Brandon shares the legend of the city underneath California's Death Valley called "Shin-Au-Av". The story originates from the Paiute Indians, and supposedly, in this mysterious underground complex, once lived an unknown race of people. The Sioux Indians also share an underground city story, in which one of their people, White Horse, accidentally found an underground dwelling occupied by strange humans. These underground humans gave White Horse a mystical talisman capable of melting rocks.

There are numerous stories from all over the world describing the existence of underground cities, complexes, and tunnels. The two most famous hidden underground cities are Agharta and Shambhala, with the supposed entrance to the first at the South Pole. Nazi Germany spent enormous amounts of money looking for the two, and it's suggested that they actually found Agharta. There, live tall, blonde, and blue-eyed people.

The ancients even possessed maps of a world before the transition to the current age. On those maps, Antarctica isn't covered by ice and the above sea land mass is much larger. The Piri Reis Map and the Oronteus Finaeus Map, among others, are said to originate from those ancient maps.

The New Testament too expresses the idea of ages, but according to Erich von Däniken, the notion is lost in translation and the following passage is plausibly inaccurate.

> *"Teaching them to observe all things whatsoever I have commanded you: and, lo, I am with you always, even unto the end of the world. Amen."* — (Matthew 28:20)

The word, world, in the above passage is mistranslated. If correctly converted from Greek to English, the word would be "aeon". So, the passage should read:

> *"Teaching them to observe all things whatsoever I have commanded you: and, lo, I am with you always, even unto the end of the aeon. Amen."* — (Matthew 28:20)

The end of this epoch isn't the end of human existence or the end of the planet—the end days. It's only the end of this type of human living and being. The popular Christian understanding is placed within one era, this age, and not within the four. The fashionable interpretation isn't complete but presented as whole.

The parable of the statue composed of gold, silver, bronze, iron, and clay, seen by Nebuchadnezzar in his dream (Daniel 2: 31-45), too describes this cosmic cycle. The fifth element, the clay, references the grand cycle the four ages are contained within. The cycle of the four ages eventually ends and then is re-established. There are cycles within cycles and all cycles come to an eventual end. Yet, only to start again. God retracts creation and then, once again, expands creation.

> *"This image's head was of fine gold, his breast and his arms of silver, his belly and his thighs of brass, his legs of iron, his feet part of iron and part of clay."* — (Daniel 2: 32-33)

Fortunately, as dark as this age is, the Sons of God incarnate, every so often, to help the human race. They will come again and again, until humanity returns to the Garden of Eden—the epoch of perfect existence—the Golden Age. (The Garden either symbolizes the Golden or it represents a state of being as a pure spirit and free of a body).

There once were Sons of God, sanctioned by the Great-Giver to rule. With the introduction of this epoch, no more they are. However, the memory of their Heavenly right to rule still remained. Soon after the Sons of God ascended, people from around the world, to legitimate their claim to kingship, exploited this memory and pretended to be the Sons of God. Nevertheless, those who claim kingship, in this day and age, are without the Divine right to rule.

> Most areas of the world where the remains of post flood civilizations are located, such as the Indus Valley (Punjab), Iraq, Iran, Egypt, Ireland, etc. experience underdeveloped conditions and/or constant conflict. This doesn't allow the nurturing of ancient knowledge and the archaeological evidence that supports this wisdom. Is this a coincidence, or purposely so to conceal humanity's history from the modern person?

The Tree of Knowledge

To eat from the Tree of Knowledge of Good and Evil is to fall, and to completely enter the physical realm. The spirit falls before the body and the body rises to govern the time and space of thought.

The physical dimension of a person is what experiences good and evil, pain and pleasure, hate and love, lies and truth, etc. The spirit doesn't. The spirit is pure and above the contradictions.

> *"But of the tree of the knowledge of good and evil, thou shalt not eat of it: for in the day that thou eatest thereof thou shalt surely die."* — (Genesis 2:17)

A constitution, in which the body is the lord and the spirit a prisoner, is considered dead by the ancient spiritual masters. And caged to this epoch, cosmic forces love the body and rain down like sunshine. Billions walk about dead in mind—billions are slaves to the body and spiritually blind—billions require the teachings of the Christ.

To the practitioner of enlightened conduct, your soul is forever tatted with a mark of divine distinction.

Why Sex is Sin

Sex is considered a sin when the orgasm is wasted. The "Big O" contains a person's spiritual potency. It's an energy source. When this energy is released, a person's spiritual potential and the likelihood of a celestial experience drastically decrease. The Saints suggest that a person cannot have both, sexual pleasure and Heavenly interactions.

The orgasm is a source of immense energy, and when harnessed, it's able to gift the spirit with Herculean strength. Nonetheless, even if it isn't harnessed, it's still required by the mind and body to optimally function. When the Big O is released, the mind and body no longer have access to essential energy and the person's vitality suffers.

The Antichrist

The popular translations of the antichrist commonly point to a person with power. Many American Presidents, many Popes, many conquerors were labelled the antichrist. However, as written of in *the New Testament*, the popular depictions are inaccurate.

The New Testament does speak of the antichrist but doesn't point to a person with power. Instead, the antichrist is considered anyone who doesn't believe in the Christ or pretends to be a Christ.

> *"For many deceivers are entered into the world, who confess not that Jesus Christ is come in the flesh. This is a deceiver and an antichrist."* — (2 John 1:7)

> *"And every spirit that confesseth not that Jesus Christ is come in the flesh is not of God: and this is that [spirit] of antichrist, whereof ye have heard that it should come; and even now already is it in the world."* — (1 John 4:3)

> *"Little children, it is the last time: and as ye have heard that antichrist shall come, even now are there many antichrists; whereby we know that it is the last time."* — (1 John 2:18)

Now, why were certain powerful people targeted as the antichrist? It's simple. It's a tactic used by influential people to assassinate the character of other powerful people and to prevent the common person from siding with their ideas. Moreover, many Christian denominations constantly preach that the end-of-days has cometh. The appearance of the antichrist is an indication of this end. To validate their end-of-days propaganda, these Christian denominations invent associations.

In the game played by those who rule, the common person is simply a pawn on a life-size chessboard.

The Beast

The Book of Revelation is not to be taken literally—it's full of symbols. If you do, nothing but confusion will ensue. The wisdom and lessons hidden within will be missed. It'll be like a bird who thinks that water is its natural habitat. Or a person who lives on Earth but thinks he or she resides on Mars. There is a thin line between what reality is and what it isn't.

Due to the wrong context, two popular concepts readily misunderstood are the two beasts written of in *Revelation*. The first beast comes from the sea and the second beast comes from the Earth.

> *"And I stood upon the sand of the sea, and saw a beast rise up out of the sea, having seven heads and ten horns, and upon his horns ten crowns, and upon his heads the name of blasphemy."* — (Revelation 13:1)

> *"And I beheld another beast coming up out of the Earth; and he had two horns like a lamb, and he spoke as a dragon."* — (Revelation 13:11)

Without going into the many popular misinterpretations, I'll dive right into it and present my understanding of the beasts.

The first beast, rising out of the sea, symbolizes a person trapped to the influences of their body, as opposed to a person who validates Godly living and strives to allow the spirit within to dominate thoughts and actions. The influences of the body are what question the existence of The Great Architect—the body strictly recognizes a material living. The influences of the spirit affirm The Lord and encourage a person to live spiritually.

The second beast, rising out of the Earth, represents the darkness of Maya/Mammon—the material world—the great illusion—the matrix. This beast is a false Christ and it offers a phony salvation. The material realm conditions people to think that the highest life purpose and the highest salvation are attained by bowing before Maya. However, materialism is forever blind to the spirit.

The second beast and the first beast have a relationship, and the second is constantly provoking the beast within the person, and the beast within the person is constantly interacting and enhancing the matrix.

Each person must battle the beasts and the first war is an internal conflict between the body and the spirit—between the lower self and the higher self. The first war is also the only that matters. The foremost battleground is within a person. If a person can defeat the first beast, the influences of the second beast will automatically perish from the time and space of thought. The second beast falls when the first beast is slain.

So, what does this mean for "the mark of the beast"? It is written that the mark will appear on the forehead or the right-hand.

Every misunderstanding leads to another and the mark of the beast is most likely only perceivable by the spiritual adepts. Every person emanates a magnetic field, or what some call the aura, and it changes frequencies and appearance in relation to the manner a person thinks and behaves. Those who think and behave as Jesus emanate a specific aura, and those who worship the material realm emanate a certain aura. Nothing can be hidden, even if the physical aspect of a person is concealing it. The invisible presence of a person is like an open book, to those who can see it. The mark is most likely a specific subtle emanation concentrated in the area of the forehead or the right-hand.

A person's magnetic field changes to reflect a person's state of awareness, and it also influences an individual's thoughts, actions, health, luck, and the type of experiences he or she will attract. The stronger a person's aura, the higher degree of positively he or she will encounter, and the stronger the magnetic field, the less negative entities are able to influence the subtle nature of an individual.

To speak a prayer, one written by a person through whom God spoke, strengthens the magnetic field. A true prayer contains Heavenly vibrations. The saintly writer combined specific sounds together to make celestial sentences.

Specific sounds power-up the subtle self and as does functioning through the beautiful half of the mind, good deeds, selflessly serving humanity, visiting sacred places (especially where Earth Energy Lines intersect), pondering and meditating on The Lord, and spending time amid the truly saintly—if you can find them.

A person's magnetic field is weakened by operating through the ugly half of the mind, by spending time amid people and places with a low frequency (such as clubs and bars), and by negative experiences. A weak field is very dangerous. It not only attracts negative experiences, the dark influences of the invisible realm might penetrate a person's sphere of existence. Once they do, they will provoke a person to continue to generate a low frequency.

Everything that lives requires energy to live. The dark entities of the invisible, those outside the perception of the five senses, are no different, but their energy source isn't the same as the human. They feed on the type of energy emanated by low vibrations. A weak magnetic field is a source of nutrition for them.

There is a realm of life outside the human five senses. Be wise as serpents. In this invisible kingdom live a diversity of creatures. Some are predatory and some are gentle. The vulturous creation loves the beast within the person. The energy the beast generates is conducive to their existence.

Chemicals can also contaminate the magnetic field and attract predatory creatures. Drunkenness—extreme intoxication—weakens the field. Moreover, as suggested by Manly P. Hall, alcohol stimulates the opening of a specific gland in the brain. Through this gland, invisible entities can enter and influence Thought Energy. A person, who blacks-out after drinking too much, is typically under the influence of a predatory creature. Either a person has left their body, during the black-out, or they're completely subdued by the predatory influence. That is why, during the blackout, he or she behaves more through the five thieves of the mind. This is also the cause of their memory loss.

If placed outside pre-Christian spiritual understanding, and read through literal eyeglasses, fantastical interpretations can be had after studying *Revelation*. If ideas are misunderstood, time is wasted, energy is misspent, and the God seeker doesn't progress.

Before I end, some consider "the Dragon", mentioned in *Revelation*, as a third beast. And this could be. However, I think popular interpretation has missed the mark and the Dragon represents this epoch and this era's characteristics. We are currently in the darkest of all four ages, known as the Iron Age, and cosmic forces readily love the first two beasts.

....

A portion of the population is abandoned to the predators. It's as if the predators must be fed or there might be devastating consequences. Or, it's their reward for performing given tasks. This is all speculation. I don't know the truth of the matter. But I do know that if an individual eats right, thinks right, behaves right, prays right, speaks right, walks right, connects right, visits right, sleeps right, and so on, a person's magnetic field will grow strong and able to resist and repel predatory creatures.

Succubus

As a child, a few times, it was suggested to me, by very wise people, that to indulge in anger, lust, attachment, the ego, and greed only harms the self. No matter how justified a person might feel about their anger, lust attachment, the ego, and greed.

Back then, I didn't heed their warnings. It all sounded so hocus-pocus. How can those elements of me possibly harm me?

Well, I was mistaken then and after many years of research, I finally understand. Swimming in anger, lust, attachment, the ego, and greed weakens the magnetic field. A weak field brings about negative experiences, repels the angelic, attracts predatory things, and unwittingly, it facilitates the manifestation of a succubus.

Sometimes, the person is behind a predatory thing. Sometimes, emotions are so powerfully projected that they create a succubus—an invisible thing that provokes the emotions and thoughts that created it, within the person who facilitated the succubus's birth. The succubus requires that type of energy to maintain an existence. Yet, it's without a complex nature. Like a jellyfish, it's a very simple creature. It has one goal, to live. It's unable to comprehend the host's agony and cognitive torture. It isn't built with the tools to do so.

The human being has the power of creation within and the succubus is an example of this. Sometimes, the person is responsible for the predatory thing haunting her or him. Sometimes, many succubuses are birthed. Yet, this understanding can be applied in the opposite sense. Function through the beautiful half of the mind and create "things" that provoke and feed on the energy produced by love, truth, humility, selflessness, and compassion.

666

I guess the next question is—What about 666?

> *"Here is wisdom. Let him that hath understanding count the number of the beast: for it is the number of a man; and his number is Six hundred threescore and six."* — (Revelation 13:18)

The popular Christian interpretation suggests that the alphabetical value to the number 666, decoded, will reveal the name of the beast, who is said to be a person. But unfortunately, many names can be derived through this method. Thus, this can't be the correct interpretation.

I'm yet to decide what 666 actually represents, but I'm confident that the propagated version isn't correct. The following are a few notions that make more sense than the number corresponding to the name of a person. The first two align with my interpretation of *Revelation*.

Researcher, Rex Bear, after reading through the Gnostic literature, believes that 666 signifies 6 protons, 6 electrons, and 6 neutrons, and represents matter—the body—the first beast. As I mentioned early on, just because I cite a particular researcher, doesn't mean I agree with all their conclusions and associations.

The pre-Jesus nations, such as the Egyptians, used the number 6 to represent incompleteness and the number 7 to signify completeness. Some theorists suggest that triple 6 represents an extremely incomplete state of being—the first beast—a primal person in whom the three aspects (the mind, body, and spirit) are not aligned to the Will of Heaven.

Numerologists believe 666, if seen by a person, is a sign for the person to reflect on their inner workings and thoughts. Under the roof of Numerology, 666 also references the number 9. 6+6+6 =18, and 1+8 =9. The number 9 is said to be a sacred number.

If the first two concepts are correct and 666 points to an incomplete individual, one trapped to matter—a beast, an archetype presented earlier, then, *Revelation 13:18* can be taken at face value. In this case, many, many millions adorn the number. They quite possibly outnumber those without the mark.

Mike Bhangu

Three Days

After a person is prepared, it takes three days of spiritual activity to free Thought Energy from the influences of the body. It takes three days to conquer the beasts. After three days, the outcome is a mystical experience. This results in the resurrection of the spirit. The spirit was free and alive before it descended into the body. The body, if enslaved to Mammon, cages the spirit. In such a state, the spirit is considered dead until it rises above its captor.

In an allegorical fashion, the following passages refer to these three days.

> *"And Joseph answered and said, 'This is the interpretation thereof: The three baskets are three days: Yet within three days shall Pharaoh lift up thy head from off thee, and shall hang thee on a tree; and the birds shall eat thy flesh from off thee.' And it came to pass the third day, which was Pharaoh's birthday, that he made a feast unto all his servants: and he lifted up the head of the chief butler and of the chief baker among his servants."*
> — (Genesis 40:18-20)

The Pharaoh represents the spirit.

> *"And I have said, I will bring you up out of the affliction of Egypt unto the land of the Canaanites, and the Hittites, and the Amorites, and the Perizzites, and the Hivites, and the Jebusites, unto a land flowing with milk and honey. And they shall hearken to thy voice: and thou shalt come, thou and the elders of Israel, unto the king of Egypt, and ye shall say unto him, The Lord God of the Hebrews hath met with us: and now let us go, we beseech thee, three days' journey into the wilderness, that we may sacrifice to the Lord our God. And I am sure that the king of Egypt will not let you go, no, not by a mighty hand."* — (Exodus 3:17-19)

Egypt represents the body and the body's rule over the time and space of thought. The land of milk and honey symbolizes an existence with the spirit as the captain of Thought Energy.

> *"And Pharaoh said, Who is the Lord, that I should obey his voice to let Israel go? I know not the Lord, neither will I let Israel go. And they said, The God of the Hebrews hath met with us: let us go, we pray thee, three days' journey into the desert, and sacrifice unto the Lord our God; lest he fall upon us with pestilence, or with the sword. And the king of Egypt said unto them, Wherefore do ye, Moses and Aaron, let the people from their works? get you unto your burdens."* — (Exodus 5:2-4)

Israel symbolizes the spirit, the Pharaoh the body, and the pestilence and the sword represent extreme suffering and an arduous trial.

> *"...for we shall sacrifice the abomination of the Egyptians to the Lord our God: lo, shall we sacrifice the abomination of the Egyptians before their eyes, and will they not stone us? We will go three days' journey into the wilderness, and sacrifice to the Lord our God, as he shall command us. And Pharaoh said, I will let you go, that ye may sacrifice to the Lord your God in the wilderness; only ye shall not go very far away: intreat for me."* — (Exodus 8:26-28)

The Egyptians represent the body's influences. The wilderness represents an environment unwelcoming to the body.

> *"And Moses stretched forth his hand toward heaven; and there was a thick darkness in all the land of Egypt three days: They saw not one another, neither rose any from his place for three days: but all the children of Israel had light in their dwellings. And Pharaoh called unto Moses, and said, Go ye, serve the Lord; only let your flocks and your herds be stayed: let your little ones also go with you."* — (Exodus 10:22-24)

The three days of darkness in the land of Egypt equates to three days of ignoring Maya.

> *"And it shall be, if thou go with us, yea, it shall be, that what goodness the Lord shall do unto us, the same will we do unto thee. And they departed from the mount of the Lord three days' journey: and the ark of the covenant of the Lord went before them in the three days' journey, to search out a resting place for them. And the cloud of the Lord was upon them by day, when they went out of the camp."* — (Numbers 10:32-34)

In these three days, The Father will be a guide.

> *"Then Joshua commanded the officers of the people, saying, Pass through the host, and command the people, saying, Prepare you victuals; for within three days ye shall pass over this Jordan, to go in to possess the land, which the Lord your God giveth you to possess it."* — (Joshua 1:10-11)

The land represents the body, and it takes three days of specific spiritual practice to become complete master over it.

> *"And it came to pass after three days, that the officers went through the host; And they commanded the people, saying, When ye see the ark of the covenant of the Lord your God, and the priests the Levites bearing it, then ye shall remove from your place, and go after it."* — (Joshua 3:2-3)

In this passage, the Ark of the Covenant represents a spiritual guide, or a spiritual marker, or possibly The Holy Ghost, who appears after three days.

> *"Now the Lord had prepared a great fish to swallow up Jonah. And Jonah was in the belly of the fish three days and three nights."* — (Jonah 1:17)

Jonah in the belly represents three days of isolation.

> *"For as Jonas was three days and three nights in the whale's belly; so shall the Son of man be three days and three nights in the heart of the earth. The men of Nineveh shall rise in judgment with this generation, and shall condemn it: because they repented at the preaching of Jonas; and, behold, a greater than Jonas is here."* — (Matthew 12:40-41)

> *"And he charged them that they should tell no man of him. And he began to teach them, that the Son of man must suffer many things, and be rejected of the elders, and of the chief priests, and scribes, and be killed, and after three days rise again."* — (Mark 8:30-31)

Three days of specific spiritual activity and a person will rise after which. In these three days, a person will experience immense suffering.

> *"And there arose certain, and bare false witness against him, saying, We heard him say, I will destroy this temple that is made with hands, and within three days I will build another made without hands."* — (Mark 14:57-59)

Three days of specific spiritual activity are required to conquer the influences of the body.

> *"And Saul arose from the earth; and when his eyes were opened, he saw no man: but they led him by the hand, and brought him into Damascus. And he was three days without sight, and neither did eat nor drink. And there was a certain disciple at Damascus, named Ananias; and to him said the Lord in a vision, Ananias. And he said, Behold, I am here, Lord."* — (Acts 9:8-10)

> *"And their dead bodies shall lie in the street of the great city, which spiritually is called Sodom and Egypt, where also our Lord was crucified. And they of the people and kindreds and tongues and nations shall see their dead bodies three days and an half, and shall not suffer their dead bodies to be put in graves. And they that dwell upon the earth shall rejoice over them, and make merry, and shall send gifts one to another; because these two prophets tormented them that dwelt on the earth."* — (Revelation 11:8-10)

Three days after a person is prepared. Three days before a rebirth. Three days of a spiritual trial by a metaphorical fire and a person will transform into a superhuman.

The story of Jesus' burial and resurrection too expresses a three-day spiritual journey. After a person is prepared to embrace the three days, at the end of three days, their body's influences will permanently quiet and the spirit will surge and influence Thought Energy. This is the true meaning of a rebirth.

> *"And that he was buried, and that he rose again the third day according to the scriptures..."* — (1 Corinthians 15:4)

Among other secrets, the specific spiritual activities of these three days, after a person is ready, I cannot reveal. It's a dangerous three days and there are truths I cannot share. Actual death is a possibility. But rest assured, if you seek The Holy Ghost, and if The Father is pleased, the knowledge will mystically appear. You will conquer the beasts.

In the story of Guru Nanak, there too is a three-day journey. It is said that he was underwater, and lost, for three days before he re-emerged as a Christ. I'm sure if we look closely at the stories of the other spiritual masters, we'll find a three-day parable.

Conclusion

Religions covet untruths and present them as absolute. This has led many reasonable people to step away from religion. Some decided to walk an institution-less spiritual path, and others, unwittingly, turned their back on The Great Architect. Unable to distinguish between religious inaccuracies and The Formless, before examining the other religious doctrines to possibly fill-in the blanks created by the corruption, they claim that the entirety of religions are out-to-lunch and people as Jesus are false constructs.

Betrayal has inspired many persons to the cave of the agnostic. Some managed to crawl back out and others are still stuck in the darkness. Until a Divine intervention or thoughts reach an absolute conclusion, the cave will remain a truth within the mind of the betrayed.

To provide the first is not in my power, but with the second, I hope the notions I unveil helped. Know that there is more to existence than this physical experience. Know that in the beginning, there was The Great End. Know that in the end, there will be The Great Beginning.

If my interpretations don't sit well with you, I apologize. My intention isn't to offend anyone. Perhaps, I'm completely mistaken. Nevertheless, I think I present reasonable conclusions worth considering. I hope they help you further your understanding, or at least, provide a wind strong enough to further lift your spiritual kite.

Appendix A: The Khalsa

Sometimes, a noble army rises. Sometimes, the righteous ones come together and battle the wicked. Among the Sikh people can be found such an organization, and amid them is the greatest covenant of the past 1000 years, the Khalsa. Established in 1699 by the Great Gobind Singh, the Khalsa is an armed union that exists for the purpose of defending against all tyrannical powers, protecting dharma, and protecting the holy of all religions—without taking anything in return. To this effect, death is a companion of the Singh (a member of the Khalsa). There is no compromising. Puran Singh, a renowned Sikh academic writes in his book, *Spirit of the Sikh*:

> *"Death, apparent death, is embraced by The Khalsa as no lover ever embraced his sweetheart. The Khalsa dies like the dashing waves of the sea, creating in the wake of its death millions more like itself. The life-breath of The Khalsa thus is losing its apparent life to gain its life everlasting."*

> *"In the ideal of The Khalsa, one can see the Ideal spirit of the passionate love of death for the sale of life as is seen in the Bushido of the Samurai of Old Japan. In that fervour of Yamoto, the physical life turns all into a little moth flickering its wings in infinite impatience to die. Death is the bride of the brave."*

Max Arthur McAuliffe, in his book, *The Sikh Religion: Volume 1*, writes, *"...no superiority of the enemies in number, no shot, no shell, can make his heart quail, since his Amrit (baptism) binds him to fight single-handed against millions."* Rightfully so, the tyrants of the world are as strong as a million giants, and those brave enough to stand against them like the Biblical "David". Only without fear, and a will to sacrifice everything worldly, can the giants be defeated.

Not only is the Khalsa a community of warriors, the Khalsa is also a community of saints. Each member is humble, kind, gentle, loving, peaceful, fearless, forgiving, God-oriented, communally aware, soft-spoken, rational, truthful, mentally disciplined, knowledgeable, poetic, worldly, and detached from the self and Maya. The Khalsa only unsheathes the sword as a shield and not for secular gain. Puran Singh once wrote:

> *"Once it is said The Khalsa occupied the throne of Delhi when the Mughal Emperor submitted and acknowledged the power of The Khalsa, the leader Jassa Singh said—'Ah! The Khalsa is atit (untouched by Maya). What has it to do with thrones'—and gave the throne back to the Mughals."*

> *"No one need be afraid of The Khalsa of Guru Gobind Singh, that it would ever think of seeking the bones of material objects. The eyes of The Khalsa are fixed heavenward."*

As dictated by Guru Gobind Singh to the great Sikh scholar, Bhai Nand Lal Goya, Goya writes in his book, *Tankhahnama*:

> *"The Khalsa is he who protects the poor, who destroys the wicked, who recites the Name, who fights the enemy, who concentrates his mind on the Name, who is detached from all other ties, who rides the horse, who fights every day, who bears arms, who promotes dharam, and who dies for his faith."*

The famous Sikh historian, Rattan Singh Bhangu, writes in his book, *Pracheen Panth Prakash*, the following on the Khalsa's creation.

> *"The perfect Guru, the Tenth, created the Khalsa Panth in this manner, so that they must wage a war against oppression."*

Guru Gobind Ji further describes the Khalsa as *"he is whose heart burns unflickering the Lamp of Naam, day and night, know him the Khalsa, the pure!"* As recorded by Puran Singh.

This connection to the essence of God is the reason the Khalsa's history is full of Singhs able to overcome incredible odds and achieve superhuman deeds, akin to those performed by Banda Singh, Deep Singh, Hari Singh, and Jassa Singh. As the Jedi draws power from the Force, the Singh draws power from the Lamp of Naam (the Primal Energy that pervades within all known and unknown).

An 18th century Muslim historian, and an enemy of the Sikhs, Qazi Nur Mohammad, once wrote of the Khalsa and the Khalsa's spirit:

> *"Do not call the Sikhs dogs, because they are lions and are courageous like lions in the battlefield. How can a hero, who roars like a lion be called a dog? Like lions they spread terror in the field of battle. If you wish to learn the art of war, come face to face with them in the battlefield. They will demonstrate it to you in such a way that one and all will shower praise on them. If you wish to learn the science of war, O swordsman, learn from them. They advance at the enemy boldly and come back safely after action. Understand; Singh is their title, a form of address for them. It is not justice to call them dogs; if you do not know Hindustani language, then understand that the word 'Singh' means a lion.*
>
> *Truly, they are lion in battle, and at times of peace, they surpass in generosity. When they take the Indian sword in their hands they traverse the country from Hind to Sind. None can stand against them in battle, howsoever strong he may be. When they handle the spear, they shatter the ranks of the enemy. When they raise the heads of their spears towards the sky, they would pierce even through the Caucasus. When they adjust the strings of the bows, place in them the enemy killing arrows and pull the strings to their ears, the body of the enemy begins to shiver with fear. When their battle axes fall upon the armour of their opponents, their armour becomes their coffin.*

The body of every one of them is like a piece of rock and in physical grandeur every one of them is more than fifty men. It is said that Behram Gore killed wild asses and lions. But if he were to come face to face with them even he would bow before them. Besides usual arms, they take their guns in hand and come into the field of action jumping and roaring like lions and raise slogans. They tear asunder the chests of many and shed blood of several in the dust. You say that musket is a weapon of ancient times, it appears to be a creation of these dogs rather than Socrates. Who else than these dogs can be adept in the use of muskets. They do not bother even if there are innumerable muskets. To the right and the left, in front and towards the back, they go on operating hundreds of muskets angrily and regularly.

...Besides their fighting, listen to one more thing in which they excel all other warriors. They never kill a coward who is running away from the battlefield. They do not rob a woman of her wealth or ornaments whether she is rich or a servant. There is no adultery among these dogs, nor are they mischievous people... There is no thief amongst these dogs, nor is there amongst them any mean people. They do not keep company with adulaters'... Now that you have familiarised yourself with the behaviour of the Sikhs, you may also know something about their country. They have divided Punjab amongst themselves and have bestowed it upon every young and old."—Jang Namah (1765)

Jang Namah is an eye-witness account of Ahmed Shah Durrani's invasion of Punjab, in the year 1764. Commissioned by Ahmed Shah, the author naturally compromises objectivity when describing events and the people the Afghans invaded. When reading his work, it's clear Nur Mohammed held a strong prejudice toward the Sikhs. He refers to them as dogs, dirty idolaters, fire worshippers, etc. Nevertheless, even with his biases, he was unable to prevent his pen from glorifying the Khalsa and the Khalsa's members.

Jang Namah also shares the story of Baba Gurbakhsh Singh Shaheed and the 30 Singhs who battled 30 000 Afghanies. The 31 fought to prevent the desecration of the Golden Temple.

The true Singh, a replica of Gobind, is able to harness Naam because those who serve the Khalsa serve God. The Khalsa is a union of the Pure (the spiritually liberated), and sanctioned by The Lord for the purpose of ushering in the "Kingdom of God." An era on earth the Singhs call the "Khalsa Raj", in which God, truth, equality, justice, freedom, and righteousness prevail. It's said that so long as the Singh is true to the principles of the Khalsa, God will protect the Singh. However, The Great Architect is quick to abandon those who forget.

According to author, Narain Singh, in his book, *Guru Gobind Singh Re-told*, a year prior to the creation of the Khalsa, Guru Gobind withdrew into the Naina Devi Hills to meditate. He sought to connect with God and request The Eternal's guidance. He was troubled by the fact that he was forced to resort to violence to combat violence. He was aware that violence is an evil that destroyed human values and an idea that contradicted the core teachings of Sikhie—love and non-violence. However, the Mughals, in their quest to convert all of India to Islam, unleashed hell on the people of India. Only those who unsheathed the sword were able to retain their non-Islamic identity. Guru Gobind unsheathed out of necessity, and even though each battle resulted in his victory, he fully recognized that violence is unbecoming.

Gobind eventually united with The Formless One, and after his union, Gobind proclaimed, as written in his book, *Bachittar Natak*:

> "The Lord has sent me into the world for the purpose of spreading Dharma. He said to me, 'Go and spread Dharma (righteousness) everywhere, seize and smash the evil doers.' Know ye holy men, I have come solely for the purpose of bringing about Dharma, saving holy men and completely uprooting wicked men."

After his union, Guru Gobind established the Khalsa and initiated the quest to restore the conditions of an honourable existence. Conceived as a champion of dharma, the Khalsa is sanctioned by The Eternal to unsheathe but only in the face of extreme evil, and when peace is useless.

Sometimes, a noble army rises. Sometimes, the righteous ones come together and battle the wicked. Among the Sikh people can be found such an organization, and amid them is the greatest covenant of the past 1000 years, the Khalsa. Established in 1699 by the Great Gobind Singh, the Khalsa is an armed union that exists for the purpose of defending against all tyrannical powers, protecting dharma, and protecting the holy of all religions—without taking anything in return. To this effect, death is a companion of the Singh. There is no compromising.

....

"Says Kabeer, those humble people become pure - they become Khalsa - who know the Lord's loving devotional worship.||4||3||" — (Ang 655 of 1430, Sri Guru Granth Sahib Ji)

 Canada Council for the Arts   Conseil des arts du Canada

BBP acknowledges the support of the Canada Council for the Arts, which last year invested $153 million to bring the arts to Canadians throughout the country.

Nous remercions le Conseil des arts du Canada de son soutien. L'an dernier, le Conseil a investi 153 millions de dollars pour mettre de l'art dans la vie des Canadiennes et des Canadiens de tout le pays.

 Conseil des arts du Canada   Canada Council for the Arts

Books by Mike Bhangu

  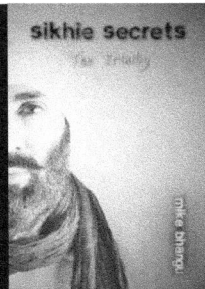

www.ingramcontent.com/pod-product-compliance
Lightning Source LLC
Chambersburg PA
CBHW070758020526
44118CB00036B/1920